Was Codex Sinaiticus Written In 1840!

J. A. Moorman

Was Codex Sinaiticus Written in 1840!
Copyright © 2018 by Jack A. Moorman
All Rights Reserved
Printed in the United States of America
August, 2018

ISBN 978-1-7321746-2-7

All Scripture quotes are from the King James Bible.

No part of this work may be reproduced without the expressed consent of the publisher, except for brief quotes, whether by electronic, photocopying, recording, or information storage and retrieval systems.

Address All Inquiries To:
THE OLD PATHS PUBLICATIONS, INC.
142 Gold Flume Way
Cleveland, Georgia, U.S.A.
Web: www.theoldpathspublications.com
E-mail: TOP@theoldpathspublications.com

The cover of this book was designed by The Old Paths Publications, Inc. Faded into the background is a page from Codex Sinaiticus. It indicates a large bracketed area indicative of where Mark 16:9-20 is missing. The picture is an illustration of a scriptorium where manuscripts were copied.

DEDICATION

To Christian J. Pinto:

A fervent defender of the King James Bible and its underlying Text. His documentary presentations through the medium of *Adullam Films* have been an eyeopener to many. He appears to have been the first in these current times to have uncovered the true nature of Codex Sinaiticus. May God continue to bless his gifted ministry.

J. A. Moorman
September, 2018

WAS CODEX SINAITICUS WRITTEN IN 1840!

PREFACE
Was Codex Sinaiticus Written In 1840!

What the Newspapers Reported:

Worldwide newspaper coverage greeted the 1933 London arrival of Codex Sinaiticus. The following was from the *Sydney Morning Herald.*

CODEX SINAITICUS
On View at Museum.
INSPECTED BY 3500 PEOPLE.
LONDON, Dec. 27. 1933

The Codex Sinaiticus, within a red and gold enamelled box, wrapped in cotton wool and brown paper, arrived at the British Museum this morning.

Dr. Bell, Keeper of Manuscripts, spent two hours testing its authenticity, after which it was installed in the entrance hall, where a queue speedily formed. About 3500 people inspected the manuscript, 80 per cent, of them placing a contribution, sometimes a Treasury note, in the box alongside.

Visitors generally were amazed at the wonderful state of its preservation and the clearness of the script. Mr. Ernest Maggs, who negotiated the sale, says: "The Soviet Government at first asked £500,000, but when real discussions commenced the price was reduced to £200,000. At £100,000 it was a wonderful bargain."

Sir George Hill, director of the British Museum, says that sentimentally the Codex is beyond the value of the Elgin marbles, Which is placed at £1,500,000.

Note the amazement at its "wonderful state of preservation" and it being a "wonderful bargain" at £100.000. That today is about Seven Million Pounds. ***THEY PAID TOO MUCH* !**

J.A. Moorman

These are strange days, but for those who believe there are good reasons to hold to the King James Bible and the Text upon which it is based, nothing is stranger than the account of a forgotten but now re-emerging debate that took place after the 1844 "discovery" of Codex Sinaiticus. It now appears that the *HOUSE OF CARDS* upon which the Modern Version text is based is far weaker than we could have imagined. Unlike other Biblical controversies, much of what we know about this one appeared in the British press; mainly in 1862 and 1863.

TABLE OF CONTENTS

DEDICATION 3
PREFACE 5
Was Codex Sinaiticus 5
Written In 1840! 5
TABLE OF CONTENTS 7
OUTLINE 9
CHAPTER 1 11
   AN IMMEDIATE PROBLEM FOR SINAITICUS 11
CHAPTER 2 15
THE UNEXPECTED PROMPT THAT REOPENED THE DEBATE 15
CHAPTER 3 19
CONSTANTINE TISCHENDORF'S ACCOUNT 19
CHAPTER 4 27
A THREEFOLD WITNESS AGAINST THE ANTIQUITY OF SINAITICUS 27
   B. WHAT KALLINIKOS OF ALEXANDRIA SAID 61
CHAPTER 5 91
A SURGE OF VATICAN "INTEREST" IN TISCHENDORF AND SINAITICUS 91
CHAPTER 6. 101
FURTHER QUESTIONS, FACTS AND FORENSICS 101
CHAPTER 7 117
FROM WHAT DID SIMONIDES COPY? 117
CHAPTER 8 123
THE COLLAPSE OF THE MODERN VERSION TEXT: .. 123
CONCLUSION 125
INDEX OF WORDS AND PHRASES 129
ABOUT THE AUTHOR 135

OUTLINE
EIGHT AREAS OF SPECIAL INTEREST

I	AN IMMEDIATE PROBLEM FOR SINAITICUS
II	THE UNEXPECTED PROMPT THAT REOPENED THE DEBATE
III	CONSTANTINE TISCHENDORF'S ACCOUNT
IV	A THREEFOLD WITNESS AGAINST THE ANTIQUITY SINAITICUS

      A. WHAT CONSTANTINE SIMONIDES SAID
      B. WHAT KALLINIKOS OF ALEXANDRIA SAID
      C. WHAT J.E. HODGKIN OF LIVERPOOL SAID

V	A SURGE OF VATICAN "INTEREST" IN TISCHENDORF AND SINAITICUS
VI	FURTHER QUESTIONS, FACTS AND FORENSICS
VII	FROM WHAT DID SIMONIDES COPY?
VIII	THE COLLAPSE OF THE MODERN VERSION TEXT: NO COHESION, NO PROVENANCE, NO PROLIFERATION, NO SINAITICUS AND PROBABLY NO VATICANUS

CHAPTER 1
AN IMMEDIATE PROBLEM FOR SINAITICUS

An example of how tenuous the common view is for the antiquity of Codex Sinaiticus can be seen by noting the following dates **1844,1855,1859,1862**.

May 1844 sees the young textual scholar, Constantine Tischendorf "discovering" portions of an apparently ancient manuscript on a visit to the Sinai desert monastery of Saint Catherine's. The well-known story of how he found it in a large waste basket and ready to be burned is itself mired in controversy. The circumstances he related are viewed with suspicion by even his most ardent supporters, including F.J.A. Hort the chief architect of the revised text of the New Testament (J.K. Elliott, *Codex Sinaiticus and the Simonides Affair*, p. 15).

The codex appeared to be an astounding discovery – a very old uncial (large lettered) manuscript in pristine condition! Tischendorf with other authorities confidently, and despite its remarkably good condition, dated the find to about 350 AD. "Here at last" in the rising demand for a new Greek text was a "second pillar" alongside the other "ancient" manuscript, Codex Vaticanus at the Vatican Library. Textual critics were able to claim that they now had the two oldest New Testaments in the world. "What better foundation could there be for a revised Greek text!" Few seemed to be bothered by the total lack of *provenance* for these two manuscripts. Why no history? Why no mention of the steps they took from AD 350 to their current resting place. Also, why is such good condition? Why no copies made of them in their travels? Also, did they really travel from 350 AD Alexandria!?

Nevertheless, with this development the prospects looked increasingly promising for a work of revision that would replace the Received Text of the King James Bible. In the years following the renown of Codex Sinaiticus and its founder Tischendorf grew immensely. However in **1855** a seemingly unrelated incident took place that had the potential to seriously impede the work of revision and deal a fatal blow to the antiquity of Sinaiticus. A seller of manuscripts and highly skilled calligraphist (also accused of being a forger!), Constantine Simonides, came to Leipzig University with a Greek manuscript of the apocryphal *Shephard of Hermes*. This for textual scholars was a cause for great excitement as all known copies of this work (written originally in the second century AD) was only known to exist in Latin. The University immediately published it. They should have looked before they leaped! It was a fake and merely a translation of a 14th or 15th century Latin copy. And, who was at the forefront in declaring and demonstrating it to be a fake? *Constantine Tischendorf*!

Two years later in **1859** Tischendorf was to find himself in a state of shock, disbelief and denial. He returned to Sinai to retrieve further portions of Codex Sinaiticus. What does he find bound at the end of the manuscript - in the *same* hand writing, with the *same* ink, and on the *same* vellum as in the preceding leaves? Virtually an identical Greek copy of the *Shepherd of Hermes* that Simonides had presented at Leipzig!

What now! What applies to the one must apply to the other. The Simonides and the Sinaiticus *Shepherd* were one and the same. As Tischendorf had so strongly pronounced the *Shepherd* published at Leipzig as being a recent forgery, what must that say about the same *Shepherd* that is an integral part of his Codex Sinaiticus? What must that say about the body of the manuscript? It can only betray that it too is recent.

With fifteen years of progress toward the revised Greek text and now increasingly so, what must he now do! In his excellent and profusely documented, *The Forging of Codex Sinaiticus*, Bill Cooper makes the following points: as "the grammar, syntax, vocabulary and numerous medieval

CHAPTER 1:

Latinisms, shouted out that the Simonides and Sinaiticus *Shepherd of Hermas* were both written in modern Greek. Tischendorf was forced to back-pedal quickly and that it was after all a very ancient Greek Text, perhaps even the original. It was one of the most audacious acts...ever perpetrated on the academic world...But instead of condemning his dishonesty almost the entire academic world closed it ranks around him and agreed with him" (Cooper, p. 46). Cooper (p. 50) says, "It was in the Preface, Prologue and Appendix of Dressel's second edition of *Patrum Apostolicorum Opera*, 1867, that Tischendorf did his back-pedalling."

By contrast J.K. Elliott (pp. 10,12) quotes a "minimal" statement by Tischendorf concerning his change of mind and does not himself mention the implications (*Journal of Sacred Literature*, July 1859). Sinaiticus must be kept afloat at all costs!

We can be absolutely certain that rather than resort to this embarrassing climb-down, Tischendorf would have tried to show, if he could, that the *Shepherd* was only an "attachment" by a much later hand. He could not! He knew well that it was an integral part of that section of the codex: same ink, same vellum, same handwriting etc.

Tischendorf was now in for another surprise; once again he was going to be troubled by Constantine Simononides. In the **13th August 1862** edition of the *Manchester Guardian*, a letter was printed from Samuel Tregelles to F.J.A. Hort. Tregelles from the conservative side and Hort from the liberal were by this time at the forefront in the push for a revised Greek New Testament. Among other matters, Tregelles wrote: **"I believe I need hardly say that the story of Simonides that he wrote the MS** [Codex Sinaiticus] **is as false and absurd as possible**." Cooper (p. 50) points out that apart from "a small circle of scholars", this astounding claim from Simonides was unknown, but "in the national press now it was in the public arena. Tischendorf was thunderstruck." (Emphasis, here and hereafter is mine).

As much as we are opposed to the textual views of Tregelles and Hort, we must agree that for a man, in fact a young man of only nineteen or twenty, to claim to be the author of Codex Sinaiticus and even call it *Codex Simonides* sounds at first hearing to be *as false and absurd as possible*. However, given Simonides' proven association with the *Shepherd of Hermes* that is bound at the back of Sinaiticus (and that is only the beginning!), I think that a reading of his initial statement to the press and the great deal that he wrote afterwards will convince many that he knows far too much about the subject to allow his detractors to dismiss him out of hand as a fabricator. Given the widespread press coverage of his interaction with leading literary and textual critics THERE IS TOO MUCH HERE TO FABRICATE! It borders on being impossible to believe that he invented the story. More absurd still is the idea put forth by J.K. Elliott, that Simonides was driven to develop the story because of an anti-German feelings and thus an anti-German attitude toward Tischendorf. See page 180 of Elliott's account.

Having mentioned J.K. Elliott, we now note:

CHAPTER 2
THE UNEXPECTED PROMPT THAT REOPENED THE DEBATE

The chief source of the available correspondence is *Codex Sinaiticus and the Simonides Affair* by J.K. Elliott (1982). It is a substantial and invaluable compilation for anyone wishing to pursue what was said at the time. My copy was purchased from Biblio.com (books@biblio.com). The author who has long been a defender and developer of the Critical Text (based primarily on the two manuscripts Sinaiticus and Vaticanus), is Professor of New Testament Textual Criticism at the University of Leeds. Dr. Elliott clearly has a vested interest that nothing be allowed to impinge upon the "antiquity" of Codex Sinaiticus. Note the following from his Preface.

> "If there is one biblical manuscript and one only that the man in the street has heard of, it is likely to be the Codex Sinaiticus. The romantic story of its discovery by Constantine Tischendorf in the middle of the last century, the public appeal in 1933 which enabled it to be purchased by Britain and the prominence of its display in the British Museum have all given it a notoriety and fame above all other manuscripts.
>
> To the biblical scholar, the contents of this fourth century codex and the distinctiveness of many of its readings have made it a reference book and storehouse of textual variants, which no editor of the Greek New Testament text can ignore. It was largely because of the discovery of this manuscript that the Textus Receptus which had held sway since 1514 lost its pre-eminence as the Greek New

Testament and that a new translation of the bible was undertaken. This was the Revised Version of 1881.

No one nowadays doubts the antiquity and importance of the Codex Sinaiticus but this was not the case in the early 1860's shortly after Tischendorf had announced his discovery. In 1862 a Greek called Constantine Simonides caused a stir in ecclesiastical and literary circles by announcing that the Codex Sinaiticus which Tischendorf was claiming as an ancient manuscript was in fact a recent work, and had in fact been written in 1840 by Simonides himself." (p. 5).

CONTENTS

Preface		5
I	Sinaiticus	9
II	Simonides	26
III	Kallinikos	71
IV	Simonides the Forger	122
V	The Biographical Memoir	173
	Index	191

It may well be a work of *Providence* that we can thank two leading proponents of the Revised text, Tregelles in that day and especially Elliott in our time for bringing the Simonides story to our notice. While Elliott seeks to refute

CHAPTER 2: THE DEBATE REOPENED

Simonides we can only wonder why after so long a time with barely a mention he should have in 1982 brought the matter up again. And, done it so thoroughly! His labours were well before the current pro Simonides presentations by:

- Chris Pinto (Adullam Films)
- Steven Avery (sinaiticus.net thetextofthegospels.com/2017/03/sinaiticus-is-not-forgery-setting-stage.html)
- Bill Cooper (*The Forging of Codex Sinaiticus*)
- David Daniels (*Is the "World's Oldest Bible" a Fake?*)
- Mark Michie (textus-receptus.com)
- David H. Sorenson (*Neither Oldest Nor Best*)

Note: As the presentation given in this study is an introduction, the interested reader is strongly urged to consult the above.

Why did Elliott bother! The issue was in the press for a couple of years and then died. Nothing further was said and certainly nothing in favour of Simonides (Scrivener was against him). John Burgon the chief defender of the Traditional Text at the time said nothing in his books. Why then did Elliott expend so much effort! Is it too much to think that he was entertaining a doubt that "the matter might not be so settled after all?" Did he feel a need to buttress the evidence against Simonides? Unless one is in complete denial, if Sinaiticus falls the Revised Text falls with it. That stark fact must have occurred to Modern Version defenders who have recently entered the debate James White, Daniel Wallace and others.

Apart from his strong bias, a chief criticism of Elliott's book is that he *does a Jehoiakim* (Jer 36:23) on some of Simonides' letters, most notably his lengthy letter to the *Manchester Guardian* (21 January, 1863). Too much of what Simonides said is scattered across the book. That is fair enough, but we should also be able to see the letters in their entirety. In many cases his testimony is buried among the letters of detractors. As Simonides himself is the *Principal Witness on the Stand*, he should be allowed an uninterrupted hearing. This by a "piecing together" and recording it chronologically has been attempted in the following pages. But first, we get a sense of the story from Tischendorf.

CHAPTER 3
CONSTANTINE TISCHENDORF'S ACCOUNT

Here, Elliott relates Tischendorf's "standard" (and often challenged!) account of how he discovered the manuscript which he at first called Friderico – Augustanus. Note that the sources for Tischendorf's story were published between 16 and 31 years after the initial finding of the codex.

In 1862 Tischendorf published *Aus dem Heiligen Lande*, which gave an account of his travels in the East. In the ninth chapter he describes how he discovered Codex Sinaiticus. An earlier and briefer account is found in his *Notitia* (1860) and a fuller, later account in his *Die Sinaibibel* (1871).

According to Tischendorf's account, he was on an expedition in **1844** in search of ancient manuscripts **under the patronage of his sovereign, King Frederick Augustus of Saxony**. While staying in the monastery of St. Catherine on Mount Sinai **he was fortunate enough to discover in a basket of papers intended for burning some vellum leaves containing portions of the Septuagint. He was informed two such basketloads had already been burned.**

Tischendorf was **permitted to remove forty three of these leaves and they were eventually published in 1846 as the Codex Frederico - Augustanus** and contain 1 Chronicles, Jeremiah with Nehemiah and Esther complete. Of the other portions of this manuscript which Tischendorf saw on that visit, he was permitted only to copy one leaf. This contained the end of Isaiah and the beginning of Jeremiah and was eventually published in 1865 in his *Monumenta Sacra Inedita I*.

It was not until **1853** that Tischendorf returned to St. Catherine's, but at that time was **not able to discover the whereabouts of the leaves he had left behind**.

The third visit to the Monastery was in **1859** and was extremely profitable. On this occasion **his patron was the Emperor Alexander II of Russia** — a factor which was to be significant in the history of the manuscript. After having been in St. Catherine's for five days, Tischendorf was talking to the steward of the monastery and brought the conversation round to the topic of the Septuagint, whereupon **the steward produced from his room a manuscript of the scriptures. This turned out to be the manuscript Tischendorf had seen in 1844** and had since been searching for. That night, far from sleeping, Tischendorf examined the manuscript and discovered not only did it contain further portions of the Septuagint but (more significantly) **the whole of the New Testament, the Shepherd of Hermas and the Epistle of Barnabas**. He transcribed Barnabas that night. (Elliott pp. 9,10).

Elliott, then continues:

It may be of interest now to see how Tischendorf assessed the significance of his discovery in a supplement to the *Leipziger Zeitung* of April 17, 1859. This takes the form of a letter addressed to the Saxon Minister von Falkenstein and was sent by Tischendorf from Cairo on March 15,1859. A translation appeared in the *Journal of Sacred Literature* in July 1859:

CHAPTER 3: CONSTANTINE TISCHENDORF'S ACCOUNT

"The kindness shown to me by your Excellency on my departure from my native land, makes it my agreeable duty to address to you the first account of a very important literary discovery which the Lord's good hand has vouchsafed to my new investigations in the East. You know **what weight the learned world attaches to the famous Vatican MS. of the Bible, and how it has for centuries been esteemed one of the special treasures of the Papal library**: you are aware how anxious men have been, and how difficult they have found it, to collate even single passages, **how earnestly Mai's edition, undertaken by order of the Pope, had been looked for since <u>1828</u>, and how gladly it was at last received, at <u>Easter 1858</u>**, after thirty years delay.

If I should now say that Providence has preserved in the corner of the so - often ransacked cloisters of the East, a MS. which may rank with the Vatican in regard to its character, extent, and age, and which on some accounts claims the precedence of it, I shall not be surprised if some doubt my skill, and the questions be put — Is it indeed true? Is it even possible? And yet as I held in my hands for the first time the precious leaves, in a convent chamber at the foot of Moses Mount (Ghebel Mousa), my own astonishment and wonder were as great as can be imagined.

The MS. of whose discovery I inform you consists of **346 fine and fair parchment leaves of so large a size that two of them have required a whole gazelle skin. The writing, upon each leaf and arranged in four columns, is of the most ancient character**, and is mostly (and especially on the outside of the skin)' preserved with **wonderful distinctness**, but **on the flesh side it is sometimes less legible,** and much more difficult to decide respecting **the numerous and**

certainly very ancient corrections to which the Codex has been subjected.

Such MSS. confessedly never have a date. It is the problem of palaeography, by careful attention to all the peculiarities of each separate MS. from the character of the letter-forms employed, from the interpunction, from the use of initials, and subscriptions, and inscriptions: from the parchment, from the tints of the ink, the old corrections, etc., to ascertain more or less satisfactorily its antiquity. **As to this MS., there scarcely was need a date to fix its century, for that it was written in the fourth century can be confirmed by all the arguments which have any weight** in palaeographic science, almost beyond all question.

The Vatican Codex goes back to the same century in my opinion and that of other able men. **The only other** Greek parchment MS. to which I had before given a chronological place prior to the Vatican, was the **Leipsic Codex Friderico - Augustanus**, but this, as I am already convinced, is a relic of the very MS. of which I am so happy as to find these important constituents.

This MS. still contains, first, considerable portions of the Old Testament, namely, most of the greater and lesser prophets, the Psalms, Job, Jesus - Sirach, Wisdom, and several other Apocryphal books. These are followed by the entire New Testament. And herein lies the extraordinary significance of the discovery. **Only three extensive Biblical MSS.** of high Christian antiquity have come down to us from the fourth century to the ninth. The most comprehensive among them is **the London Codex Alexandrinus, which wants** almost the whole of Matthew's gospel as well as considerable part of 2 Corinthians, and two chapters of John's gospel. **From the Vatican MS. still more is absent**, namely, the Apocalypse and four Pauline epistles

CHAPTER 3: CONSTANTINE TISCHENDORF'S ACCOUNT

altogether, with a third part of the epistle to the Hebrews. **But of the MS. of the New Testament now found, not a single leaflet is wanting!** It is moreover the only one among the MSS. of the New Testament of a thousand years old and upwards, which is complete. The divine who knows the importance attached to the MSS. of that age, in the endeavour to fix the apostolic text, will accept this as a principal authority. It is a new pledge of the possibility of deciding and restoring the genuine apostolic text, to which this doubtless is a close approximation, as to the main features of it. I only add that my examination of the MS. convinces me of **its perfectly coinciding in age with the Vatican Codex.**

      I have yet to name two other component parts of the same MS., the discovery of which alone would have sufficed to make my, new journey fortunate and successful. Next to the Bible, the most precious literature of the church is the writings of the apostolic fathers. We have but few remains of this class, and these few are for the most part often in doubtful texts, imperfect, or only extant in translations. It is thus with the so-called **Epistle of Barnabas**, which, if not composed by a companion of Paul, must have been written very soon after the end of the first century. It is quoted both by Clement and Origen, in the second and third centuries, as even a part of Holy Scripture, and still later, such writers as Eusebius, refer to it as among the doubtful books of the Canon. This epistle is equal in extent to that to the Romans; **several MSS. of it have been found before, but all are modern**, and in all alike the first five chapters are wanting, of which the text can be gathered only through a very corrupt Latin version. How great then was my wonder when I found the whole of Barnabas in this MS., at the close of the Revelation: I could not lay the volume down till I had read and copied the whole text. Divines will no longer have to read from the uncertain

Greek text of late MSS., and a faulty Latin version, the epistle which in the second Christian century was so reverently handled and highly prized.

In the height of my joy at this discovery I was to have a last surprise. I found a **separate portion of fifty-two columns**, with the inscription «The Pastor;» it was the first part of **the Pastor of Hermas**, also pertaining to the second century, and likewise claiming a kind of apostolic regard. **Till recently, its Greek text was thought to be lost**. This MS. proves that in the earliest times both Barnabas and Hermas were reckoned as constituent parts of Scripture by some, if their authority was also doubted. **Of Hermas, Simonides confessedly brought a very perfect Greek text to Leipsic, part copied by him from a MS. at Mount Athos, and part upon three paper leaves of the fourteenth or fifteenth century. After this text was published in December 1855, and repeated soon after by me more accurately, considerable doubt arose about it, whether it was really ancient or a mediaeval translation from the Latin. I especially opposed the last view and my opinion is confirmed by these leaves, at least 1000 years older, shewing that the Leipsic text had been derived from the original but is corrupt and that in consequence of a mediaeval use of the Latin.**

I am glad that the scientific mission committed to me by the Russian Government, and promoted by you, has at its outset so noble a literary discovery as its result. Relying upon the Imperial favour, I venture already to set before the learned world the hope of the publication of the MS. **A carefully revised copy of its 132,000 columnar lines will be completed by the beginning of April**, if God permit. The Vatican MS. was known 300 years before many cherished wishes were gratified in its publication.

CHAPTER 3: CONSTANTINE TISCHENDORF'S ACCOUNT

> It may perhaps need only so many years instead of so many centuries to enrich the Christian literature with that most precious document now discovered.
>
> Constantine Tischendorf. (Elliot pp. 10-12).

We will come back to Tischendorf in Chapter V, but note again two key statements at the beginnings of the above accounts:

> According to Tischendorf's account, he was on an expedition in **1844** in search of ancient manuscripts **under the patronage of his sovereign, King Frederick Augustus of Saxony**. While staying in the monastery of St. Catherine on Mount Sinai **he was fortunate enough to discover in a basket of papers intended for burning some vellum leaves containing portions of the Septuagint. He was informed two such basketloads had already been burned.**
>
> Tischendorf was **permitted to remove forty three of these leaves and they were eventually published in 1846 as the Codex Friderico — Augustanus......**

And, Tischendorf at the beginning says:

> You know **what weight the learned world attaches to the famous Vatican MS. of the Bible, and how it has for centuries been esteemed one of the special treasures of the Papal library**: you are aware how anxious men have been, and how difficult they have found it, to collate even single passages, **how earnestly Mai's edition, undertaken by order of the Pope, had**

been looked for since 1828, and how gladly it was at last received, at Easter 1858, after thirty years delay.

Tischendorf's story has raised many questions. It has often been asked how the monks could have been so careless as to have allowed an ancient *vellum* copy of the Scriptures to be *in a basket of papers intended for burning*. Others have pointed out that vellum does not burn well and would have filled the monastery with a stench. Often overlooked is **1828**. On this date the Pope declared that Codex Vaticanus would be published. This was shortly after the death of King Frederick Augustus I of Saxony (an area of eastern Germany on the border with Poland). Though Saxony was strongly Protestant, its kings where Catholic. It was the name, King Frederick Augustus II that Tischendorf first gave to Codex Sinaiticus.

CHAPTER 4
A THREEFOLD WITNESS AGAINST THE ANTIQUITY OF SINAITICUS

A. WHAT CONSTANTINE SIMONIDES SAID

Before looking at what Simonides said we should first get a brief overview of the man himself, and the unique and controversial personality that he was. The following from *Wikipedia* states that **his literary activity was extraordinary**.

Simonides was born on the small Greek island of Symi, on the coast of the Aegean Sea in 1820, and died in Egypt of leprosy.

He lived in the monasteries on Mount Athos **between 1839 and 1841** and again in **1852**, during which time he acquired some of the Biblical manuscripts that he later sold. He produced a great number of manuscripts ascribed to Hellenistic and early Byzantine periods. He allegedly forged a number of documents and manuscripts and claimed they were the originals of the Gospel of Mark, as well as original manuscripts of poems of Homer. He sold some of these manuscripts to the King of Greece. Greek scholars exposed what some claimed to be forgeries quickly and he left Greece and travelled from country to country with his manuscripts. He visited England **between 1853 and 1855** and other European countries, and **his literary activity was extraordinary**. Some of his works were published in Moscow, Odessa, in England, and in Germany. He also wrote many other works which were never published.

From 1843 until 1856 all over Europe he offered for sale manuscripts purporting to be of ancient origin. He created a considerable sensation by producing quantities of Greek manuscripts professing to be of fabulous antiquity – such as a *Homer* in an almost prehistoric style of writing, a lost Egyptian historian, a copy of St. Matthew's Gospel on papyrus, written fifteen years after the Ascension, and other portions of the New Testament dating by him to the first century. These productions were later claimed to be forgeries. [Not absolutely proven, see next page].

In 1854 and 1855 Simonides tried unsuccessfully to sell some manuscripts to the British Museum and the Bodleian Library. Thomas Phillips was a less critical purchaser and bought for the Phillips Library at Cheltenham some manuscripts. In **1855** he visited Berlin and Leipzig. He informed Wilhelm Dindorf that he owned a palimpsest of *Uranius*.

On **3 September 1862**, in an article of *The Guardian*, he claimed that he is the real author of the Codex Sinaiticus and that he wrote it in **1839, 40**. According to him it was "**the one poor work of his youth**". According to Simonides, he visited Sinai in 1852 and saw the codex. Henry Bradshaw, a scholar, did not believe his claims.

Simonides questioned many of official scientific positions accepted by scholars. He did not respect any scholars. He interpreted Egyptian hieroglyphics in different ways than Champollion and other Egyptologists. He tried to prove that his method of interpreting Egyptian hieroglyphics was superior. He placed the death of Irenaeus at 292 (c. 130 – c. 200).

CHAPTER 4: A THREEFOLD WITNESS AGAINST ANTIQUITY

Also, in many other complicated questions he had his own, usually controversial, point of view, but **after ascribing the authorship of the Codex Sinaiticus to himself, the rest of his credibility was destroyed by the British press.**
https://en.wikipedia.org/wiki/Constantine_Simonides

By far the largest section of Elliott's work, 50 pages, is chapter 4 which deals with Simonides' reputation as a forger. Whatever his rights or wrongs may have been, these pages demonstrate that he possessed an extraordinary skill and was capable of astonishing output. He had a wide reputation for his abilities as a scribe of "ancient" texts. The following from ***The Anthenaeum* (16 February, 1856)** gives a sense of this.

This put an end to Simonides' career in the East. He left Constantinople, and came to England; and, in spite of the repeated warnings addressed to all Public Libraries, he succeeded in disposing of many of his MSS. Among the most curious MSS. which he left in England, one is a copy of *Hesiod*, another, the identical copy of some books of *Homer*, sent from Chios to Hipparchus, the son of Pisistratus. It is almost incredible that such impudent frauds could have been successful; but there is little doubt that many more will now be brought to light. **The British Museum is said to possess thirty MSS. of Simonides. These may possibly be genuine; yet they would require a new and careful examination** (Elliott p.170).

These fifty pages compiled by Elliott can be brought to bear on the question of whether Simonides was capable of producing Sinaiticus or at least a substantial part of it. His widespread reputation pointed to the likelihood that he could. It should also be noted that on the question of forgery, Simonides had his defenders, most notably J.E. Hodgkin, curator of the Mayer Museum in Liverpool, and a journalist, Charles Stewart who in 1859 published, *A Biographical Memoir of Constantine Simonide*. This was written before the Sinaiticus story broke and deals only with his life generally and accusations of forgery. As the opening line says:

> The sole object of the following pages is to vindicate the reputation of a friend, most unjustly assailed by calumny (Elliott p. 174).

Thus, whether for better or worse, in Constantine Simonides we are dealing with a significant personality. As a native Greek speaker, however, he was handicapped in this debate by his dependence upon translators for the publication of his twenty or so letters to the British press. He spoke on a number of occasions of the difficulty and complained also of mistranslation. (See below his letters of 14 January and 4 February, 1863). We will also see from the following that the final sentence of the *Wikipedia* overview is wrong!

> …..after ascribing the authorship of the Codex Sinaiticus to himself, the rest of his credibility was **destroyed** by the British press.

When Simonides is given *HIS DAY IN COURT AND ALLOWED AN UNINTERRUPTED AND CHRONOLOGICAL TESTIMONY*, the British press while generally against him editorially, will have in fact preserved the record that he gave. I think that many reading this full record will come to the conclusion that he was telling the truth. Further, when the manuscript's forensic evidence is added to his testimony, the case is frankly *overwhelming*!

CHAPTER 4: A THREEFOLD WITNESS AGAINST ANTIQUITY

Here then are fourteen of the key Simonides letters that the British press published.

Simonides ONE, 3 May 1859: Reference to *The Standard*. This introduction to an unavailble letter by Simonides appeared later in *The Guardian* (date not given)

…..Having seen the *Standard* of Monday, May 23, 1859, an account of the discovery at Mount Sinai, 1 wrote to **Kallinikos** on the subject, and received from him a letter on which unfortunately I cannot now lay my hand, but which I will publish if I should hereafter find it. This letter, however, not being sufficiently explicit, **especially as regards the identification of the newly found» Codex with my own**, I wrote to him again for a more circumstantial statement, which he gave in the following letter. C.S. (Elliott p. 88).

Simonides TWO, 4 January, 1860: A letter to his biographer Charles Stewart, part of which was used in his "Initial Account letter" fourteen months later. It appeared later in the *Guardian* (date not given). His supporters believe that this previous letter corrects several of the mistranslations in his letter of 3, September 1862.

CONCERNING SIMONIDES' VISIT TO ST.CATHERINE'S IN 1852

1. In 1844 I was again at Constantinople, and went to the island of Antigonus to see the Patriarch Constantius, and give him an important packet of MSS. I was received with his usual courtesy, and in the course of conversation I asked about my transcript of the Scriptures. He replied, «**Long ago, my son, I sent thy valuable work to Sinai**». **And twice have I seen it myself in the Library of Sinai, first in 1844 and then**

in <u>1852</u>. 1 asked the librarians how and whence the Library had obtained it. They having nothing to say (neither the first nor the second knowing anything about it), were silent, and I said nothing to them about the transcription; but taking it in my hands found it somewhat altered in form, both externally and internally, for it had an older appearance than it ought to have had, and the MS. was defective in part. As I remembered the dedication to the Emperor Nicholas (which I had prefixed to the book in golden characters), and found that it had been taken out, I smiled, and replaced the book in its original place, and commenced my philological investigations (for there were in that library many very valuable MSS), and pursuing them with diligence I discovered many things of great importance, among which the most important were all the pastoral writings of Hermas, and the Holy Gospel according to St. Matthew, and the disputed epistle of Aristeas to Philocrates (as I have elsewhere remarked), all written upon Egyptian papyrus, principally in the first century, together with some other important MSS. which I described in a letter to Constantius, as also to my spiritual father Catlistratus, Archbishop of Libya, on my return to Alexandria.

2. **Dionysius, the professional calligrapher** of the monastery, was requested to undertake the work, but he declined, saying that he could not accomplish the task assigned to him, which he considered very difficult and quite beyond his capabilities.

When he objected to perform what had been allotted to him, for the reasons which he gave, I myself yielded to the entreaties of my venerable uncle and undertook the performance of the work, **for I had been proved and approved in time past, and my hand was**

CHAPTER 4: A THREEFOLD WITNESS AGAINST ANTIQUITY

very well practised from childhood in the ancient writing.

And so **we straightway inspected the oldest MSS. preserved in Mount Athos** of the sacred writings referred to.

I for my part carefully considered the questions connected with the best possible performance of the penmanship. And the learned **Benedict** taking in his hands a copy of the **Moscow edition of the Old and New Testament** (published at the expense of the illustrious **brothers Zosimas**, and by them presented to the Greeks), **collated it, with my assistance, with three only of the ancient copies, which he had long before annotated and corrected for another purpose and cleared their text by this collation from remarkable clerical errors, and again collated them with the edition of the Codex Alexandrinus, printed with uncial letters, and still further with another very old Syriac Codex; and gave me, in the first instance, Genesis to copy** (Elliott pp. 55,56) ……

Simonides THREE, 3 September,1862: *The Guardian*, Simonides'Full Initial Account.

THE SINAI MS. OF THE GREEK BIBLE

Sir — As you have in your impression of August 13 published a letter from a correspondent signing himself F.J.A.H., in which reference is made to me, I must ask you for permission to make a statement in reply. Your correspondent favours you with some extracts from a letter written by Dr. Tregelles, in which the following sentence occurs: «**I believe that 1 need hardly say that the story of Simonides, that he wrote the MS., is as false and absurd as possible**».

The MS. referred to is that called the **Codex Sinaiticus**, now being published under the editorship of **Professor Tischendorf**, at the expense of the Russian Government. As what Dr. Tregelles calls my «story» has never been published, and as that gentleman can only have heard of it through an indirect medium, it may interest both Dr. Tregelles and your readers to have the «story» direct from myself. I will tell it as briefly as possible.

About the **end of the year 1839**, the venerable **Benedict, my uncle, spiritual head of the monastery of the holy martyr Panteleemon in Mount Athos**, wished to present to the **Emperor Nicholas I., of Russia**, some gift from the sacred mountain, in grateful acknowledgement of the presents which had from time to time been offered to the monastery of the martyr. Not possessing anything which he deemed acceptable, he consulted with the **herald Procopius** and **the Russian monk Paul**, and they decided upon **a copy of the Old and New Testaments, written according to the ancient form, in capital letters**, and on parchment. This together with the remains of the seven apostolic fathers - **Barnabas**, **Hermas**, Clement Bishop of Rome, Ignatius, Polycarp, Papias, and Dionysius the Areopagite-they proposed should be **bound in gold, and presented to the Emperor** by a common friend. **Dionysius, the professional calligrapher** of the monastery, was then begged to undertake the work, but he declined, saying that the task being exceedingly difficult, he would rather not do so. In consequence of this, **I myself determined to begin the work**, especially as my revered uncle seemed earnestly to wish it. **Having then examined the principal copies of the Holy Scriptures preserved at Mount Athos, I began to practise the principles of calligraphy, and the learned Benedict taking a copy of the Moscow edition of both Testaments** (published and

CHAPTER 4: A THREEFOLD WITNESS AGAINST ANTIQUITY

presented to the Greeks by the **illustrious brothers Zosimas**), **collated it with the ancient ones**, and by this means **cleared it of many errors**, after which he gave it into my hands to transcribe. Having then received both the Testaments, freed from errors (the old spelling, however, remaining unaltered), being short of parchment, I selected from the library of the monastery, with Benedict's permission, a **very bulky volume, antiquely bound, and almost entirely blank, the parchment of which was remarkably clean, and beautifully finished**. This had been prepared apparently many centuries ago - probably by the writer or by the principal of the monastery, as it bore the inscription...(a Collection of Panegyrics), and also a short discourse, much injured by time.

I therefore took possession of this book, and prepared it by taking out the leaf containing the discourse, and by removing several others injured by time and moths, after which I began my task. First, **I copied out the Old and New Testaments, then the Epistle of Barnabas, the first part of the pastoral writings of Hermas** in capital letters (or uncial characters) in the style known in calligraphy as….(amphidexios). The trancription of the remaining Apostolic writings, however, I declined, because the supply of parchment ran short, and the severe loss which I sustained in **the death of Benedict** induced me to **hand the work over at once to the bookbinders** of the monastery, for the purpose of replacing the original covers, made of wood and covered with leather, which I had removed for convenience - and when he had done so, I took it into my possession.

Some time after this, **having removed to Constantinople, I showed the work to the patriarchs Anthimus and Constantius**, and communicated to them the reason of the transcription. Constantius took it, and, having thoroughly examined it, **urged me to present it to the library of Sinai**, which I accordingly promised to do. **Constantius had previously been Bishop of Sinai**, and since his resignation of that office had again become Perpetual Bishop of that place.

Shortly after this, I was placed under the protection of the illustrious **Countess Etleng and her brother, A. S. Stourtzas**, by the co-operation of two patriarchs; but, before departing for Odessa, I went, over **to the island of Antigonus to visit Constantius**, and to **perform my promise of giving up the manuscript to the library of Mount Sinai**. The patriarch was, however, absent from home, and I, consequently, left the packet for **him** with a letter. On his return, he wrote me the following answer:

My dearly beloved Son in the Holy Spirit, Simonides; Grace be with you and peace from God. **I received with unfeigned satisfaction your truly valuable transcript of the Holy Scriptures- namely, the Old and New Testaments, together with the Epistle of St. Barnabas and the first part of the pastoral writings of Hermas, bound in one volume, which shall be placed in the library of Mount Sinai, according to your wish**. But I exhort you earnestly (if ever by God's will you should **return to the sacred Mount Athos) to finish the work** as you originally designed it, and he will reward you. Be with me on the 3d of next month, that I may give you letters to the illustrious **A. S. Stourtzas**, to inform him of your talents and abilities, and to give you a few hints which may prove useful to the success of your plans. I sincerely trust that you were born for the honour of your country. Amen. Constantius, late of Constantinople. — an earnest

CHAPTER 4: A THREEFOLD WITNESS AGAINST ANTIQUITY

worshipper in Christ. Island of Antigonus, **13th Aug. 1841**.

After I have received the above letter, I again went to visit the patriarch, who gave me the kindest and most paternal advice, with letters to Stourtzas after which **I returned to Constantinople, and from thence went to Odessa in November, 1841**.

In **1846** I again returned to Constantinople, when I at once went over to the island of **Antigonus to visit Constantius**, and to place in his possession a large packet of MSS. He received me with the greatest kindness, and we conversed on many different subjects, amongst others, upon **my transcript, when he informed me that he had sent it some time previously to Mount Sinai**.

In 1852 I saw it there **myself, and begged the librarian to inform me how the monastery had acquired it** but he did not appear to know anything of the matter, and I, for my part, said nothing. However, **I examined the MS. and found it much altered, having an older appearance that it ought to have. The dedication to the Emperor Nicholas, placed at the beginning of the book, had been removed**. I then began my philological researches, fort here were several valuable MSS. in the library, which I wished to examine. Amongst them I found the pastoral writings of Hermas, the Holy Gospel according to St. Matthew, and the disputed Epistle of Aristeas to Philoctetes (all written on Egyptian papyrus of the first century), with others not unworthy of note. All this I communicated to **Constantius**, and afterwards to my spiritual father, **Callistratus at Alexandria**.

You have thus a short and clear account of **the Codex Simonides, which Professor Tischendorf, when at Sinai, contrived, I know not how, to carry away**; and, going to St. Petersburg, published his discovery there under the name of the Codex Sinaiticus. When, **about two years ago, I saw the first facsimiles of Tischendorf**, which were put into my hand **at Liverpool, by Mr. Newton, a friend of Dr. Tregelles, I at once recognised my own work, as I immediately told him.**

The above is a true statement of the origin and history of the famous Codex Sinaiticus, which Professor Tischendorf has foisted on the learned world as a MS. of the fourth century. I have now only one or two remarks to make. The name of the professional calligraphist to the monastery of St. Panteleemon was **Dionysius** the name of the monk who was sent by the **Patriarch Constantius** to convey the volume from the island of Antigonus to Sinai was **Germanus. The volume, whilst in my possession, was seen by many persons, and it was perused with attention by the Hadji John Prodromos, son of Pappa Prodromos, who was a minister of the Greek Church in Tebizond. John Prodromos kept a coffee-house in Galatas, Constantinople, and probably does so still. The note from the Patriarch Constantius, acknowledging the receipt of the MS., together with 25,000 piastres, sent to me by Constantius as a benediction, was brought to me by the deacon Hilarion. All the persons thus named are, I believe, still alive, and could bear witness to the truth of my statement.**

Of the internal evidence of the MS. I shall not now speak. Any person learned in palaeography ought to be able to tell at once that it is a MS. of the present age. But I may just note that **my uncle Benedict corrected**

CHAPTER 4: A THREEFOLD WITNESS AGAINST ANTIQUITY

the MS. in many places, and as it was intended to be re-copied, he marked many letters which he purposed to have illuminated. The corrections in the handwriting of my uncle I can, of course, point out as also those of Dionysius the calligraphist. In various places I marked in the margin the initials of the different MSS. from which I had taken certain passages and readings. These initials appear to have greatly bewildered Professor Tischendorf, who has invented several highly ingenious methods of accounting for them. Lastly, I declare my ability to point to two distinct pages in the MS., though I have not seen it for years, in which is contained the most unquestionable proof of its being my writing.

In making this statement, I know perfectly well the consequences I shall bring upon myself but I have so long been accustomed to calumny, that I have grown indifferent to it and I now solemnly declare that my only motive for publishing this letter is to advance the cause of truth, and protect sacred letters from imposition.

In conclusion, you must permit me to express my sincere regret that, **whilst the many valuable remains of antiquity in my possession are frequently attributed to my own hands, the one poor work of my youth is set down by a gentleman who enjoys a great reputation for learning, as the earliest copy of the Sacred Scripture**s. C. Simonides. (Elliott pp. 26-30).

<u>**Simonides FOUR, 25 September, 1862**: *The Clerical Journal* (reprinted in *The Journal of Sacred Literature*)</u>

Sir, -I have no intention of replying to your criticism of September 11, nor to any of those which my letter to the *Guardian* may elicit in the public journals, until the discoverer of the Codex has endeavoured to exonerate himself from the charge of ignorance involved in my statement. Nor do I feel myself called upon to reply at all to anonymous antagonists. I have, therefore, merely to remark, that **I adhere rigidly to the narrative I have already given, which has long been in the hands of my friends, in London and elsewhere (with one of whom I find Dr. Tregelles has maintained a brisk correspondence)**, and the truth of which I have far ampler means of substantiating than you can possibly imagine. I am, Sir, your obediently, C. Simonides. (Elliott pp. 37,38).

Simonides FIVE, 10 December, 1862: *The Guardian* (reprinted in *The Literary Churchman*

Sir, - **I ascertain from letters received in the month of November last, that the hieromonachos Kallinikos of Alexandria, has written to you, refuting the antiquity of the Codex Sinaiticus, and declaring that it has been written in modern days, and by myself.** I beg you, therefore, briefly to acknowledge the receipt of it, and, at the same time, to say whether you have any intention of publishing it.

I must inform you that the above - mentioned Kallinikos is a perfectly upright and honourable man, well known for truth and probity, so that **his simplest word may be relied on. He was living at Athos when I wrote the Codex Sinaiticus (which was about 1840); he overlooked me during the progress of the work, and thus became an eye - witness of it**. His testimony may, therefore, be considered as invaluable. I am, Sir, yours truly, C. Simonides. (Elliott p. 79).

CHAPTER 4: A THREEFOLD WITNESS AGAINST ANTIQUITY

Simonides SIX, 14 January, 1863: *The Guardian*

…..Every one must admire the fair and impartial remarks appended to the letter which you did me the honour to publish on the 10th of December, 1862. It is not my fault that I have not sooner replied to **your insinuations of complicity with Kallinikos.**

In the month of November I forwarded to my friend Mr. Scott, in Manchester, for translation, my reply to the letter of Mr. Wright of 5th November, and with it a copy of one of the letters of Kallinikos, which I sent you today for publication.

I have only this day received a portion of the translation of my reply, and that of the letter has not come to hand at all, so that I am indebted to another hand for its appearance even as early as the present time.

If you will refer to the original you will find that Kallinikos (who certainly knows not a word of English) never asserts that he «read in the Guardian my letter», but that «he has read that your journal was the means of making known to the world». The way in which this came about is very simple. I wrote to Kallinikos giving him a copy of my original Greek letter from which the English translation which appeared in your journal was made, and appended the strip containing the article in English. You will see by the subjoined letter what was his reply, and why I wrote to you to ask if his letter had been received, as also I did to the *Times* and *Literary Churchman*, but am still without reply from those papers. My early connection with Kallinikos will be, in degree, ascertained by reference to his own letters. **It is not for me to bring witnesses to the respectability of a man well known in his own country**, and whom I have not brought forward as a witness, but who has written to you on his own responsibility. It is not on secondary evidence, but on that of the Codex itself, that I rely; but as his name has been associated with mine, it is right that the public should know what I am able to show them of his acquaintance with the history of the Codex.

It is quite evident that Mr. W.A. Wright does not know anything of the subjects about which he writes, as his arguments are as weak as they are malicious. I reserve my reply to him till next week, having already trespassed largely on your space. **If I had a good knowledge of the English language, neither he nor any one else would have reason to complain of the tardiness of my replies, but the necessity for translation causes great delay, and engenders many errors.** C. Simonides. (Elliott p.86).

Simonides SEVEN, 21 January, 1863: *The Guardian*, Supplement to the Initial Account. Elliott places excerpts of this lengthy letter in different parts of his book.

......You prepared yourself, my dear Sir, for the defence of the Sinaitic Codex by swallowing indiscriminately all the falsehoods concerning its discovery, told by your famous Tischendorf. But what scientific proofs have you to confirm its genuiness. Certainly none: neither do I expect such from you nor from your friend Tischendorf, for neither you nor he possess the true knowledge of Palaeographical Science. You have only learned to say at random, this is genuine, and this is spurious, but you do not know the reason. But although I possess many proofs of the spuriousness of the manuscript, I shall keep silent on these for the present. First, because **I intend to write a special work on the subject** and secondly because the Codex will prove this itself when published and the portion already published partly shows this (Elliott p.38)......

CHAPTER 4: A THREEFOLD WITNESS AGAINST ANTIQUITY

The discovery of the library induced my uncle to establish a printing -press at Athos for the dissemination of the various unpublished MSS. and those which he was preparing for publication.

For this purpose I was urged by him to go to Athens, and provide there everything requisite for printing. I went and placed myself under the direction of **A. Coromela** for a sufficient time, he **being then the first printer in Athens**, and on this account also some spoke disrespectfully of me. I wrote to my uncle from Athens duly, that it was impossible for any one to obtain a proper printing - press in Greece, because the Greeks themselves procured from France every requisite for printing. Being assured of this by others also, **he recalled me to Athos. I sailed from the Piraeus in the month of November, 1839, and landed again at Athos for the fifth time. After a few days I undertook the task of transcribing the Codex, the text of which, as I remarked before, had many years previously been prepared for another purpose. But Benedict**, as well as the principals of the monastery, wishing to recognise with gratitude the munificence of the **Emperor Nicholas** on the one hand, and desiring on the other to acquire a printing - press without expense, and being unable otherwise to effect these purposes, **decided that a transcript of the Sacred Scriptures should be made in the ancient style, and presented as a gift to the Emperor Nicholas, and he found that all the heads of the monastery perfectly agreed with him**. Accordingly, having again revised the books ready for publication, and first Genesis, he gave it to me to transcribe (Elliott, p. 30)…..

Dr. Tregells (sic) in *the Guardian* of August 13 says that in three days only he went through the MS. of the pseudo - Sinaitic Codex, examined it,

compared it with other MSS., and copied several parts. This was blindly believed by everyone, although I am sure from what he says that he possesses a very superficial knowledge of such matters. Surely if Dr. Tregelles could perform such a Herculean work in three days, **could not my uncle, a man of acknowledge learning and experience in such matters, reperuse his work while I was transcribing the book of Genesis.** (Elliott pp. 30,31)......

First [regarding a misprint in the *Biographical Memoir* by Charles Stewart regarding Simonides' birthdate], I say that my revered parents are happily still alive, and say that I was born in the year 1820, November the 5th, on Sunday, the sixth hour before noon. The circumstance is confirmed by the certificate of the priest who baptised me, who still lives, a worthy abbot in the monastery of the Taxiarchs in the island of Syme, which is erected in the ancient town called Aigle, and commonly named Michael. This certificate is countersigned by the Senators of the island of Syme, and sealed with the seal of the island, and signed also by the Austrian agent resident there. This certificate, with other documents confirming all I say, I am ready to show to any one who desires to see them. In the face of such evidence not another word need be said. (Elliott p.41. In fact Simonides did write further and to the same end concerning his birthdate in this letter. pp. 42,45)....

You adduce to us the shortness of the time as a forcible argument, saying that it is wholly impossible for any one to copy in a few months the whole pseudo-Sinaitic Codex. I admit that, according to your judgment, it may be so, but according to mine, I who am called Daedalus by some of the journals, it is quite possible, and by no means laborious; for **I could write five pages of this pseudo-Sinaitic Codex daily, and in the space of**

CHAPTER 4: A THREEFOLD WITNESS AGAINST ANTIQUITY

ten months I will give you 1,500 pages. I know that I wrote 1,205 pages in eight months and ceased from the work only because the skins failed. If you doubt this«Lo, here is Rhodes, here is the leap» according to the proverb. Deposit £10,000 sterling in my name in the Bank of England and I will write again this same work in your presence, and in presence of your friends in the same space of time. Then take the manuscript and let me take the money; but if I fail, which is impossible, I will give you such an ancient MS. as you choose from those which I possess.

Knowing this, I say to you again that the MS. of the Sacred Scriptures taken from Mount Sinai by Tischendorf, is my production, and by no means ancient.

The Codex proclaims this itself, as shall be afterwards shown when my proofs will speak for themselves. Words are therefore needless.

Truly I wonder how people can credit such unreasonable falsehoods, things wholly impossible, and believe the reports of Tischendorf — viz., that I prepared palimpsests, and wrote 10,000 pages of an Egyptian Lexicon, 7,000 pages of the Alexandrine Philological Catalogue, 10,000 pages of *Uranius*! 8,800,000 pages of various other ancient - writers on different subjects! That I corrected the corrupted texts of various classical writers, filled up many blanks of injured ancient MSS., and wrote and prepared papyri! And all this in a very limited space of time, for which work a life of two thousand years would not suffice me, had I two thousand hands, and one thousand heads. **Yet they consider it a wonder to have made a simple copy of a manuscript of the Old and New Testaments, done by me in my juvenile years.** O wonder of wonders! And also in the following issue:

I was also called the golden calligraphic pen, because I transcribed the rules of the college at Aegina in golden letters, and ornamented them with some devices. I also wrote calligraphic exercises for the instruction of my college companions; not only this, but on the death of **Charilaos, our teacher of calligraphy**.

I succeeded him with the approbation of the directors of the college, although still very young. I also transcribed the *Olynthiacs of Demosthenes* in ancient characters, and declaimed them successfully at the public examinations, for which I was designated Demosthenic Rhyme, by **Philetairos, Professor of Literature. I was also called Euclid's Compasses by Rhega, Professor of Mathematics**, an embodied Genius by my uncle, an extraordinary Phenomenon by the Patriarch Constantius, Cheirographodephet by the **Editors of the *Telegraph of the Bosphorus***, Chalkenteros by the ***Messenger of the Byzantines***, Indefatigable mind and pen by my companions, Lynceus by Dindorf, Hand of Daedalus by the **Editors of the *Athena***, published at Athens, and by many others of whom it is needless to speak at present. Alexander v. Humboldt named me «a living enigma and indissoluble Gordian knot» as C. Stewart, the journals the *Dial*, **January 17, 1862**, and *Bath Chronicle*, **March 13, 1862**, report. (Elliott pp. 58,59).....

I undertook this work, then, not as a tyro, but as one versed in the ancient writting: for before this work, as I have mentioned above, I had written the *Olynthiacs of Demosthenes* in ancient characters, and **had copied at twelve years of age the ancient inscriptions in the Aegina collection,** besides four of the services at Mount Athos in 1837 in golden letters, ancient and modern, as well as the service of St. Pantaleon in golden characters. These services, especially the professional calligraphist of the monastery, **Dionysius**,

CHAPTER 4: A THREEFOLD WITNESS AGAINST ANTIQUITY

could not imitate completely, for he was a copyist but not an archaiographer, and therefore could not execute other writing but what he had been taught from boyhood, round and clear penmanship. He was moreover, unacquainted with the ancient Greek language, and altogether ignorant of ornamentation, on which account I often wrote the ornamental work, titles and capital letters of works which he transcribed, for which he usually styled me Chrysographer, so that this good Dionysius had simply the work of transcribing the ecclesiastical books — for at Athos they generally appreciate written books more than the printed copies which come from foreign parts—but he knew not calligraphy properly although taught from childhood. And although I had a peculiar inclination for it, as well as for all the fine arts, I never became a professional calligraphist, because I had always more important and independent occupations in hand. **But I was compelled to undertake this work** — first, to gratify my uncle; secondly, as no one was there at hand at Athos to execute it; and thirdly, which was the most important to me, in the hope of obtaining the present of a printing - press. To these motives may be added my youthful ambition to become first of all at Mount Athos in the profession of calligraphy, which actually came to pass.

On account of all these circumstances I undertook the work, and began immediately after the resignation of Dionysius to study the principles of calligraphy as much as was needed. (Elliott pp.59,60).....

I learned the art of preparing suitable materials for writing — the proper ink, the making of bone pens, the polishing of the skins, the cleaning by chemicals of a few leaves soiled by time, the careful and proper division of the columns, the adoption of the style of writing, and such other things as are proper to archaeography. All these things belong to the graphic art. (Elliott p. 61).....

If you understand the twofold significance of the note which exists at the end of the fourth column of the eighth page of the pseudo - Friderico - Augustine Codex [earlier name given to Sinaiticus at Sinai], you would repent of what both you and your patrons have stirred up against me inconsiderately. (Elliott p. 50. Unknown location within 21 January letter)....

What, then, have you to oppose to the evidence of living men occupying the exalted rank of priesthood, O zealous defender of the pseudo -Sinaitic Codex? Other testimony I shall adduce after a little, and shall prove palpably the folly of yourself and patrons. Do you disbelieve the attestations of the Patriarchs, Archimandrites, and monks of the Eastern Church? If you are still incredulous, I say to you, remain faithful in your faithlessness. And I, for my part, by no means care from henceforth about this. **I have proclaimed the truth**, although well I know that such truth has both very great and disagreeable results. It behoves me, however, to speak, because my conscience itself, and education, which even Mr. Tischendorf admires as shown above, and the Church to which I belong - viz., the Greek, occupying the first rank among the Churches from which the grace of truth issued and spread abroad - do not permit me to conceal the truth in any manner; **for I will answer as I should to the All-seeing God in the Day of Judgment. Therefore I said I have spoken, I have no sin**-Wholly yours. C. Simonides. (Elliott p. 87).

CHAPTER 4: A THREEFOLD WITNESS AGAINST ANTIQUITY

Simonides EIGHT, 28 January, 1863: *The Guardian* **(and in** *The Literary Churchman*,

....**I was taught the means of knowing the ancient MSS. of every period** and of every nature of their changes from time, also the knowledge of the skins, and the chemical preparation of the different writing — inks and the effects of the atmospheric changes of the different climates of the world. Further, I acquired the knowledge of the preparation of the skins of every city of the ancient nations, and such other information as is requisite with regard to the indisputable evidence both of the spuriousness and genuiness of MSS. of every kind; which information it is to be regretted is not possessed by any of the archaeologists and palaeographers of our day, as I was sufficiently assured by many circumstances, first and last, and more especially lately when the pseudo Sinaitic Codex appeared. (Elliott p. 61).....

Benedict died at the time Mr. Stewart says, and I set out to Syme after three months for the sake of dispelling my grief on the death of my uncle, bringing with me, in a ship belonging to my family, the manuscript library to my father's house. Thence I went to Constantinople, and again returned to Mount Athos, after a few days; but the words never left out of my hands until the skins failed. Afterwards **I added my corrections** which my uncle had made, and returned the second time to Constantinople from Athos.

For this reason the writing and ink vary a little; many of the notes being written with different ink and pens, and with less care. (Elliott p 64) ......

Simonides NINE, 2 February, 1863: *The Literary Churchman*

Dear Sir, — **Tischendorf speaks falsely if he says that he did not see the Pentateuch, for the Old and New Testaments were all contained in one volume. I saw them in safe preservation when I was at the monastery in <u>March, 1844</u>**, a little before Tischendorf's arrival. And, when I was there a second time (<u>in 1852</u>), **I again saw my MS., but uncared for, and altered and lacking a part, and full of marks**, **unskillfully written by a later hand; and the dedication to the Emperor Nicholas was also missing. But the Pentateuch was still there** — all right; the proof of which is, that **I took a tracing from it, of four pages, containing the acrostichs**, two of which I showed to yourself, before Dr. Drakakes, and Callinikos saw it, who remarked **the acrostichs** in his letter to me. Tischendorf, in denying this, conceals an artful purpose; perhaps he intends, in some third happy visit, another «discovery» which he may present to Queen Victoria, or the Emperor of the French (Elliott pp. 51,52).....

<u>Simonides TEN, 4 February, 1863:</u> *<u>The Guardian</u>* <u>(reprinted in</u> *<u>The Journal of Sacred Literature</u>*<u>)</u>

....Mr. W. A. Wright is again in error in asserting that I stated at Cambridge that my age was fifteen years when I wrote the Codex. What my interpreter may have said I know not, who speaks very fluently many things which he knows about me, and also his own opinions, but I do know that I was never asked the question at all. The only mention of fifteen years in that conversation was in relation to the age of the modern MS. of Esdras, one of the three MSS. which I particularly consulted in writing the text and notes upon those books.

The errors which seem to arise on both sides from the necessity of an interpreter **make me very sorry that there are not more gentlemen in England, among**

CHAPTER 4: A THREEFOLD WITNESS AGAINST ANTIQUITY

all those who profess to be acquainted with ancient Greek, who can understand me when I speak in that language. In Cambridge I only had the pleasure of meeting one such — viz., the Rev. W. M. Gunson, M. A., Professor of Greek in Christ's College, to whom, with the Rev. John Hays, M.A, and many other gentlemen, especially of this college, I was indebted for extremely kind, hospitable and courteous treatment, during my stay in Cambridge. (Elliott p.43)......

Mr. Bradshaw's very proper and natural query - **«How is it possible that a MS. written beautifully, and with no intention to deceive, in 1840, should in 1862 present so ancient an appearance?» -1 answer simply thus: -The MS. had been systematically tampered with, in order to give it an ancient appearance, as early as 1852**, when, as I have already stated, it had an older appearance than it ought to have had; and from what 1 then was, I am not surprised that Mr. Bradshaw should have been deceived in his estimate of its age.

Again, I seriously assert (as Mr. Bradshaw seems to think 1 am jesting on this grave subject) that I wrote the Codex, to portions of which Tischendorf has given the names of Friderico - Augustanus and Sinaiticus; and **I challenge him to produce these Codices in London. I will meet him there at any time he may appoint, and in a public meeting of literary men assembled for the purpose it shall be once and for ever decided whether he or Simonides has spoken truly.** (Elliott p. 68)......

Simonides ELEVEN, 16 February, 1863: *The Literary Churchman*

To the Editor of the Literary Churchman, SIMONIDES SENDS GREETING.

It is true that I understood, at the time, almost nothing of the arguments which, against truth, against probability, and with bitter feeling, were urged against me, at the meeting of the Royal Soc. Literature, by my enemies of the British Museum; so that I gave no reply, though I had a great deal to say. I will now answer concisely, and will give a categorical reply if the Secretary of the Society will furnish me with a copy of the Report.

Thou knowest that nothing reasonable was advanced by my opponents, and that their arguments are held as vain by those who are not of their school; and that the Chairman finally dissolved the meeting without anything definite having been proved, either about the Papyri or the Codex Pseudo - Sinaiticus, although the Report of the Council was very decided, containing many things which I can show from the printed Report, to proceed from men not thoroughly acquainted with the matters of which they wrote.

I shall confirm the genuineness of the letters of Kallinikos by convincing proof, and then **I shall prosecute Mr. W. A. Wright for libel**; for, as is said in the writings of the ancients. (Elliott p. 102)…..

Simonides TWELVE, 11 March 1863: *The Guardian* **(Simonides, (speaking in the third person, defends the validity of his 1952 trip to Sinai)**

……If you should meet with my *Autographs,* which were published in autograph in 1854 at Odessa by the monk Callinicus, **you will read there the whole account of the family of the writer of the pseudo-Sinaitic Codex**, and not only this, but that he was at Mount Sinai, not once but twice or thrice. And should you also peruse the remarks made in pp. 9 and 16 of the

CHAPTER 4: A THREEFOLD WITNESS AGAINST ANTIQUITY

Appendix to No 1 of the Memoir, published at Munich in 1857, **you will find further confirmation of the fact that Simonides was at Sinai in 1852**. The same thing is established also by the *Four Theological Tracts* published by Simonides in London in 1858. (Elliott p.47)......

Simonides THIRTEEN, 16 June, 1863: *The Literary Churchman* (reprinted in *The Guardian; The Journal of Sacred Literature*)

.....I am at a loss to know whether this gentleman has been grossly imposed upon or not. But two things are perfectly clear—1st, that the negative testimony of a Kallinikos of Sinai, whose name I have never heard, and of whose existence I am doubtful, to the effect that he did not write the letters of Kallinikos of Athos, only proves the folly of those who wrote to the wrong individual; 2nd, that the letter, of which you have published a copy, is not such as would be written by a person holding the position which the correspondent of Mr. Davies is supposed to hold. **The Kallinikos who addressed the letters to the London papers on the subject of the Codex «Sinaiticus» is a Thessalonian by birth; his ancestors spring from the town of Niaousta, in Macedonia, and are related to General Karatasus. He was born in the year 1802,' and named Kyriakos. He took the name of Kallinikos on his admission to the church; and having taken an active part in the Greek Revolution, received the surname of Keraunos, on account of his bravery.** He then ceased (as is necessary, according to our ecclesiastical law, in cases wherein a priest has taken up arms), from the profession of public sacerdotal duties, and **spent a long time in a monastery of Mt. Athos, where I made his acquaintance.** Since this time he has been engaged in semi—political missions, and I have had continued correspondence with him. He has travelled through Europe, Asia, and part of Africa, and the whole of the Archipelago, and has published at Moscow and at Odessa a number of my letters to him upon Archaeological matters. What has my friend in common with the Kallinikos of Sinai? whose knowledge of the events which have occurred in his monastery seems to have been derived from a seventeen years' absence—(see his statement, that he lived away from his monastery from 1838 to 1855)—verily nothing at all. But because it suits Mr. Davies' purpose, he first discovers that there is a man of the same name as my correspondent at Mt. Sinai, takes great pains to inform us that he is «as honourable man», and then, after a long interval, prints his information, to the effect that he is quite ignorant of the matters about which he is asked. He may now, perhaps, find another Kallinikos at Cairo, or at Damascus, or where not? The name is not an unusual one.

The Archbishop even of Mt. Sinai is named Kallinikos—the late Patriarch of Alexandria was named Kallinikos—and there are several of the same name in Mt. Athos, each of whom may write him another letter, assuring him that he did not write the letters to Simonides, and that «therefore (mark the logic) they have been forged by Simonides»! It is clear that Mr. Davies must have considered that there was but one Kallinikos in the East, and that it was immaterial where he resided, so that he could be brought to deny that he wrote the letters which were written in reality by my friend Kallinikos of Mt. Athos.

It is not surprising that this Kallinikos should have been unable to hear of my three visits to Mt. Sinai from his brethren, for two reasons—1st, that divers of the monks are continually replaced by others, and are in turn sent to the possessions of the monastery in

CHAPTER 4: A THREEFOLD WITNESS AGAINST ANTIQUITY

Russia, Wallachia, Bulgaria, &c. Only some twenty or thirty monks are retained at Mt. Sinai; and so great are the changes, that on my second visit I only saw two of the same faces which I had seen during my first stay. 2nd: **I was at Mt. Athos** [This is a mistake, it should read Mt. Sinai. See 1 July letter] for political reasons, and was habited as a monk, and was known as Sophronius, and not as Simonides. These matters would be well understood by those who know the peculiar relations of the Greeks, Roman Catholics, and Turks in those regions, but may be incomprehensible to some of your readers.

I emphatically deny that the Codex Sinaiticus was inscribed in the Ancient Catalogue, for the good reason that no ancient catalogue exists; there was none there whatever, till I made a catalogue, during my first visit, for the Patriarch of Constantinople, Constantius, who before was Archbishop of Mount Sinai.

I have now said perhaps enough about the non-identity of Mr. Davies' Kallinikos and my own, though I shall be happy to give any further information which may be required as to my friend, or to satisfy any gentleman who has visited Mount Sinai, of the correctness of my assertions as to my three visits to the monastery there.

And now I must enlighten the public a little about the style of, the letters of the new Kallinikos. I say, that they are not the work of a genuine Hieromonachos living in his monastery, for these reasons: 1st, That they are not marked with the sign of the cross at the beginning and end, which is the ancient and universal custom; 2nd, It is not lawful for any of the clergy of the Greek Church to give titles of veneration to the ministers of any congregation not recognised by our church, and whoever does so is liable to severe punishment. Your readers may inform themselves upon this point by consulting Mr. Curzon's« Monasteries of the Levant». I have not the book at hand to refer to, but I remember that an instance is given therein of the ignorance of high titles in the English Church professed by Greek ecclesiastics; 3rd, It is not allowed to any monk, who is in residence at his monastery, to receive any letter from, or send any letter to any correspondent, either father or mother, unless the hegoumenos of the monastery first read such letters or reply. If an attempt is discovered to evade this regulation, the letters are burnt. All letters which leave the monastery bear, or ought to bear, the autograph note of approval of the hegoumenos. For the monks are supposed to have renounced the world and its relationships, and to need no intercourse with the outer life, and many a time epistles from father or mother, secretly given, have been discovered and forcibly taken away. The whole monastery is like a garrison, and this increases the difficulty of sending letters surreptitiously; 4th, The style of the letter is quite complimentary, and not in accordance with ecclesiastical gravity. The writer certainly answers with great good nature, exactly in the ivy tone which he could not fail to see, from the beseeching tenor of Mr. Davies' letter, would be agreeable to his correspondent; but he goes too far in politeness when he makes use of the expression quite foreign to the tongue of a Greek ecclesiastic....

That these are not genuine Greek expressions, but English or French compliments translated into our tongue, one need not be a Greek to perceive; and, indeed, the whole letter bears evident marks of translation from a foreign language; 5th, I beg your readers to observe what has doubtless escaped Mr. Davies' notice, viz. the date of his correspondent's letter—the first of April (13th, N.S.). The first of April and its absurdities are perpetuated in Greece with far more freedom than in Europe. It is the great day for amusing deceptions and delusions; the day

CHAPTER 4: A THREEFOLD WITNESS AGAINST ANTIQUITY

on which hoaxes of all sorts are perpetrated, and no man, either clerical or lay, who wished to be believed, would dream of dating his letter «the first of April». If he unwittingly did so, he would still not get his countrymen to believe he was in earnest. I cannot tell who is the deceiver in the present instance; but there can be no doubt that some one is enjoying a hearty laugh at the expense of the readers of the Guardian.

All this time too, the real test of the genuineness of the Codex «Sinaiticus» is neglected. The public were assured that in *May* Tischendorf was to be in London, armed with a portion at least of his great Codex. I have waited in England hoping to have the opportunity of meeting him, face to face, to prove him in error; but May has come and gone, and the discoverer has not appeared.

Let the favourers of the antiquity of the MS. persuade him to come at once, and brave the ordeal, or else for ever hold his peace. I am, Sir, yours respectfully, C. Simonides. (Elliott pp. 106-109).

Simonides FOURTEEN, 1 July, 1863: *The Literary Churchman* (reprinted in *The Guardian*)

Sir —**I see that a clerical error has been made by my translator in my letter to you of the 17th June, which has rather needlessly perplexed Mr. Davies, but which I hasten to correct. The context should have shown that gentleman that Mount Sinai and not Mount Athos was intended to have been mentioned** as the place in which for political reasons I changed my dress. In Mount Athos, where I was well known, there was no necessity for such disguise.

It is impossible to understand the invitation by Greek priests to an English clergyman, to come into the chancel during the time of service; as such an offer would subject him to ecclesiastical penalties according to the canons of our Church, as Mr. Davies ought to know. I concur with Mr. Davies in asking Greek scholars to decide whether the letter purporting to come from Kallinikos of Sinai does not throughout betray a foreign idiom.

Mr. Davies wants to make out that I have changed the residence of Kallinikos. It is not so. In the same letter (of Dec. 3d.) in which he is called «Kallinikos of Alexandria»—(It should have been translated «has written from Alexandria....I stated that he was living at Mount Athos when I wrote the Codex. I call him «of Mount Athos», because he is a monk of Mount Athos, **and all Mr. Davies' ingenuity cannot destroy his existence or history, or identify him with the monk of Mount Sinai.**

Mr. Davies shirks my query about Tischendorf: when is he coming?

C. Simonides. (Elliott p. 113).

In his list on page 38, Elliott mentioned five other letters that Simonides wrote to the British press. The following could not be found in his book.

- 2nd October, 1862: *The Clerical Journal:* (reprinted in *The Journal of Sacred Literature*)
- 3rd. December, 1862: *The Guardian*
- 2nd March, 1863: *The Literary Churchman*
- 13th March, 1863: *The Literary Churchman*

CHAPTER 4: A THREEFOLD WITNESS AGAINST ANTIQUITY

• 26th August 1863: *The Guardian* (reprinted in *The Literary Churchman*)

Noting especially the emphasised portions, the extensive correspondence from Simonides does not sound like a fabrication. THERE IS TOO MUCH HERE TO FABRICATE. He had placed himself under the full glare of scrutiny by the Press and leading textual and literary critics of Britain. His deliberations appear to be earnest and sincere. He seems clearly to be a party to what he is talking about. There are too many details, the cores of which are his verified tenures at Mount Athos and trips to the Sinai monastery. He speaks as having first-hand knowledge of the Codex. He even names it after himself. With the many names, places and dates the letters cannot be easily dismissed. His statement that many of the witnesses were still living invites the examination of his testimony. Further, why would he set himself up to the ridicule he knew these letters would bring? IT SEEMS HIGHLY UNLIKELY THAT HE COULD HAVE INVENTED THIS STORY!

As the academic world closed ranks to support Tischendorf's reversal on the *Shepherd of Hermss*, so they would rise to support Tischendorf against the claims of Simonides. The stakes were huge, (they are much more so today!), all the "big guns" were brought out. Yet, they do not, we believe, latch on to anything in his account that approached being a fatal error or inconsistency. Elliott cites fourteen arguments that were used against Simonides (pp. 39-66).The letters of Simonides himself (nineteen) with Kallinikos (seven) and J.E. Hodgkin (nine letters) answer very well the arguments of the opponents.

Elliott demonstrates that as respecting letters to the press, the "principal challenger" to Simonides was W. Aldis Wright, librarian of Trinity College, Cambridge. He wrote ten letters, often lengthy and dismissive. That Wright had a vested interest in this debate is shown by the fact that he "was to become engaged in the preparation with Westcott and Hort of the Revised Version of 1881; He was secretary to the Old Testament committee" (Cooper p. 38). Four others wrote one letter each in opposition to Simonides. These were: Henry Bradshaw, S.P. Tregelles, W.S.W. Vaux and W.T. Newham (Elliott pp. 36,37). Thus, by this reckoning there were thirty-five letters written in support of Simonides during the period of debate and fourteen letters against.

Of the letter writers, both Kallinikos and Hodgkin knew Simonides. Of those who had written in opposition only Henry Bradshaw, Keeper of Manuscripts, Cambridge University Library, had met Simonides. Bradshaw had seen both Sinaiticus and samples of Simonides' calligraphy of the Greek uncial text.

28 January, 1863: *The Guardian*; Henry Bradshaw's letter concerning his meeting with Simonides at Cambridge

SIR, As **Dr Simonides has cited a letter which he wrote to me in uncial characters** in October last, while he was at Cambridge, and **as I have with my own eyes seen and examined the Codex Sinaiticus** within the last few months, perhaps you will allow me to say a few words.

The note which Dr Simonides wrote to me was to convince me and my friends that it was quite possible for him to have written the volume in question, and to confirm his assertion that the uncial character of the manuscript was as familiar and easy to him to write as the common cursive hand of the present day. [Simonides had made a similar presentation to *The Guardian* on 21 January]

He had invited some of us to Christ's College to examine his papyri and to discuss matters fairly.

CHAPTER 4: A THREEFOLD WITNESS AGAINST ANTIQUITY

He could speak and understand English pretty well, but his friend was with him to interpret and explain. They first taxed us with believing in the antiquity of manuscripts solely on the authority of one man like Tischendorf, and they really seemed to believe that all people in the West were as ignorant of Greek as the Greeks were ignorant of Latin......, Cambridge, 26 January 1863 (Cooper pp. 113-117).

After this promising introduction to Simonides' challenge, Bradshaw thereafter deals with generalities. If as Tregelles said, *the story of Simonides that he wrote Codex Sinaiticus is as false and absurd as possible*, Bradshaw could now demonstrate that by comparing Simonide's uncial samples with that of the Codex. He does not say anything further about that.

B. WHAT KALLINIKOS OF ALEXANDRIA SAID

Kallinikos Hieromonachos was a Greek monk of Alexandria and friend to Simonides. He claims to have been at Athos and actually observed Simonides penning the codex that was to be a gift to Czar Nicholas I. As his testimony is crucial against the antiquity of Sinaiticus, every attempt was made to discredit him, his testimony and in fact his very existence. It was suggested by W. Aldis Wright that Kallinikos was an invention of Simonides and that it was he that wrote the following letters. In fact there is substantial proof to the contrary. Those who sought to deny any connection of Simonides with Mount Athos and the very existence of Kallinikos and Simonides' uncle Benedict were strangely silent regarding the following and significantly published catalogue compiled by S.P. Lambros.

> Spyridon Paulos Lambros, *Catalogue of the Greek Manuscripts on Mount Athos: Edited for the Syndics of the University Press,* Vol. 1 (Cambridge: University Press, 1895); and Vol. 2 (1900).

S. P. Lampros was Dean of the University of Athens, but with a PhD from the University of Leipzig he would have been influenced by the move toward revision that was sweeping Europe. He compiled a two-volume catalogue of the books and manuscripts he found on Mt. Athos with the names and dates of those who penned them. He lists the *Holy deacon and teacher Benedict* (six times), *Kallinikos Monachos* (four times), and *Constantine Simonides* (two times). The ledger entries (6405, 6406, 6407) show that Kallinikos and Simonides were at Benedict's Panteleimon monastery at Mt. Athos on 27 March, 1841. This agrees with the time stated by Simonides and Kallinkos (Daniels pp. 304-308; Cooper pp. 38-40).

J.A. Farrer quoted this exact Lampros information in 1907 (Daniels p. 307). How then could Elliott in his copious compilation omit it! Having devoted fifty pages in his Chapter III to the question of whether Simonides had a friend named Kallinikos who was at Mt. Athos; how could he have overlooked the prestigious Cambridge *Catalogue of the Greek Manuscripts on Mount Athos*?

Concerning Kallinikos' entry in the *Catalogue*, Cooper notes:

CHAPTER 4: A THREEFOLD WITNESS AGAINST ANTIQUITY

The term [of Kallinikos the monk] is of much interest because it is the same term by which Kallinikos himself signs his letters to Simonides and those he wrote in support of Simonides to the newspapers - Kallinikos the monk. It certainly belies the notion that Simonides and Kallinikos never knew each other, that Kallinikos never existed or even that Simonides forged these letters himself as was so strongly alleget by Aldis Wright *et al.* To do that, to forge Kallinikos' signature, he would have had to have known what Lambros was going to publish decades after. Simonides was clever; very clever; but he was not as clever as that (p. 38).

Kallinikos ONE. 5 August 1858; First of four letters from Kallinikos to Simonides. Written from Smyrna. The four letters survive in the Hodgkin archive of the British Library.

....**These also send thee greeting, the Deacon Hilarion, and thy friends Nicander and Niphon, who lent thee the Books of Esdras at the time when thou wast preparing in Athos, at the exhoration of my uncle, the present (of the Holy Scriptures) to the glorious Emperor Nicholas**. They also wished to know whether the work was finished, and given to the Emperor, and whether thou wert suitably required for it; because they had no certain knowledge about these matters. **I told them all about it, and how the manuscript in question is now in Mount Sinai, and how thy indifference (forgive me, my son, for this true statement of mine) frustrated the original intention.** I certified them that this MS. of the Scriptures is still preserved in Sinai (as thou also knowest), because **I saw it there with my own eyes when I was in the Monastery of St. Catherine in 1845 in the month of July**, and handled it with my own hands, and **found it**

WAS CODEX SINAITICUS WRITTEN IN 1840!

very defective, and somewhat changed and when I asked the reason, I understood from **Gabriel**, the keeper of the treasures, that **his predecessor had given the manuscript to a German, who visited the monastery in 1844 in the month of May**, and who having had the MS. in his hands several days, **secretly removed a part of it**, and went away during the time that the librarian lay ill, afflicted with a typhoid fever. Nothing more could I learn about it, but I hope (if God will) to go next year again into Egypt, and thence to Sinai, when I shall search into all things, and send the result for thy information and that of thy friends...

Farewell, my son, and pardon the garrulity of an old man. - Thy Spiritual Father, Kallinikos Hieromonachos. (Elliott p. 87).

Kallinikos TWO, 9 November 1861: Second of four letters from Kallinikos to Simonides. Written from Alexandria

+ Dear Son in the Lord, Simonides, Grace be to thee and peace from the Father, Son, and Holy Spirit, One God.

That master and pupil of all guile, and all wickedness, the German **Tischendorf**, has unexpectedly rushed into thy net: for having inspected in **the common library** (where it was found a short time ago, and where it was placed by thy spiritual father **Callistratus** when he went to Alexandria) the Codex which thou wrotest at Athos, **some twenty-two years ago**, as a present to the deceased Emperor of Russia, Nicholas I, at the request of thy wise and distinguished uncle **Benedict,** and subsequently going to Constantinople after his death **gavest unfinished to the blessed Patriarch Constantius, who sent it to Mount Sinai by the Monk Germanus** of Sinai, whom thou knowest, and which was

CHAPTER 4: A THREEFOLD WITNESS AGAINST ANTIQUITY

afterwards given to the **Hieromonachus Callistratus to be compared with the three old Codices of the Sacred Scriptures** (which thou knowest, and which are kept in the treasury), and was then disregarded because **thou didst not make thy appearance at the proper time** in Mount Sinai to transcribe it according to the earnest wish of the Patriarch, **he has proclaimed it as genuine, and as the oldest of all the known Codices in Europe** of the Old and New Testaments.

Alas for the palaeographical knowledge of such as he! And if, O my son, the sages of Western Europe take knowledge of and criticise matters in the same fashion as Tischendorf, the shallow leader of Leipzig, I must say that no true criticism or sound judgment in antiquarian matters remains there. This manuscript then being thus estimated (as very old) by the German Tischendorf, was snatched away from the monastery, was afterwards transferred to Cairo, and after a few days **was lent to Tischendorf, by the mediation of the Russian Consul in Egypt**. And it is said that the restoration of the Codex after its publication was guaranteed by the Russian Ambassador in Constantinople. But I do not believe in any promise of the Ambassador or the Consul, for the restoration of the Codex, and even if they did promise it, I do not believe that they would ever restore it to the monastery of Sinai. I judge from previous events. «For a Russian official (as the proverb says), a liar, and a thief, are synonymous». But let others treat of all this, as also of the arrangements, just or unjust, made by the Russian Consul and the guileful Tischendorf for the accomplishment of their purposes. I am not surprised at any of the circumstances, but only at the fact that this Codex, recent as it was, and thy handiwork, was ascribed to the fourth century. Here is a miracle forsooth, and yet people sneer at us for believing miracles! **This Codex, my son, I saw several times, and**

particularly three of the Acrostics which thou showedst to me at Athos when I overlooked thee in that pleasant writing -room of thine.

The first reads thus - Κ.ʿιμωνιδου χειρ ιπιραιωσε με

The second - Κ. Λ. Φ.ʿιμωνδδου Μακεδονὸ εργον διαριστον ειμι

The third - ʿιμωνιδου το ολον εργον

I also saw the fourth and fifth, but do not remember them now; and also calligraphic symbols, and especially the numerous corrections, and corrections again of these, and annotations both of thyself and of thy uncle, by which I recognised thy work; but I said nothing to any one, nor shall I speak of the matter till thou shalt request me; and for this reason have hastened to give thee the information in the present letter.

The Codex in question, as we are now quite certain, was **transported to St. Petersburg to be published, and its antiquity was established by the learned there. Now we shall see whether they will endorse the vain talking of Tischendorf, whom I have myself seen and conversed with four times, and whom I found superficial in all things, and quite ignorant of the language of our immortal ancestors.** He only chatters mechanically the Scriptures and understands their meaning by Latin versions, and not at sight; so that every ancient Greek work which has not been translated is considered by him as hard to understand, and is set down by him as being in the common Greek tongue, which the foolish critics have christened Romaic. And the questions which have been most clearly settled (about Greek palaeography) he is quite unacquainted with. In a

CHAPTER 4: A THREEFOLD WITNESS AGAINST ANTIQUITY

simple word, he deceives the world by his reputation, as thou hast before remarked. Now, it is thy business to prove and proclaim the man's real character, and to show how different it is from what it appears to be.

Farewell, O son in the Lord, and fight the good fight, and write to me sometimes, that we may hear of thy good deeds in behalf of our nation, and our mother the Church, from their author, the faithful son of his country, and not from others.

Alexandria, 9 (O.S.) November of the year 1861 Thy sincere and hearty well - wisher in the Lord, +Kallinikos Hieromonachos

P.S. - Remark this also, that the same man came on another occasion to the monastery of Mount Sinai in the year **1844, in the month of May, and there saw thy Codex, and secretly abstracted many leaves** (as I wrote to thee long ago) and went away undisturbed, (because, unfortunately, the librarian, who only could have reproved and exposed his wickedness, lay seriously ill, and departed shortly after to his rest in heaven). - Thine, Kallinikos.

Markos and **Dorotheos** and **Joasaph** salute thee; they are going tomorrow to Jerusalem, and thence to Damascus. I have received all thy books, and have given them to thy friends, therefore be at ease on that question. When art thou coming to Egypt? Thou knowest that they presence is urgently required. Come quickly, I entreat thee again, for we are on the eve of great affairs, as thou well knowest. In great haste. (Hodgkin in the 28 Jan. 1963 *Guardian* comments on this letter; Elliott pp. 88-90).

Kallinikos THREE. 5 November 1862: Third of four letters from Kallinikos to Simonides. Written from Alexandria

WAS CODEX SINAITICUS WRITTEN IN 1840!

+ My son Simonides, well-beloved in the Lord - 1 have perused the translation, or rather the Greek original, of thy letter to the Editor of the Guardian concerning the pseudo - Sinaitic Codex, and I applaud thy love of truth. But **I am sorry that thou hast omitted many circumstances not essential to the subject, and I fear, on account of the brevity of thy narration, true though it be, there will be many conjectures amongst those who are doubtful of the truth of the matter.** I myself have also written, as an eye -witness, to some of the journals of London concerning this question, among others to the *Guardian,* to whom I wrote as follows...(Here follows the text of the 3 Dec. 1962 letter written by Kallinikos to *The Guardian*).

Thus I wrote to the editor of the *Guardian*, and in almost similar terms to the others, copies of which letters I have by me, and will send to thee, if they should refuse to publish them (which, however, I can hardly believe); so that thou mayst publish them thyself. Farewell, my son, and inform me of current events. - Thy Spiritual Father,

+Kallinikos Hieromonachos. (Elliott p. 90).

Kallinikos FOUR. 6 November 1862: Fourth of four letters from Kallinikos to Simonides. Written from Alexandria

+ My Son in the Lord, Simonides—.Yesterday, the 5th November (O.S.) of the present year I wrote to thee concisely, in which letter I copied my letter to the Guardian, and I hope that thou wilt receive - it safely, for I directed it as thou didst instruct me. To day it seems to me best to send thee my letter to the *London Times*, and to the *Literary Churchman*, that thou mayest have it in thy hands for who knows what a day may bring forth? So here follow the copies, and first that of the letter to the

CHAPTER 4: A THREEFOLD WITNESS AGAINST ANTIQUITY

Times. (Here follow copies of two letters from Kallinicos to the Times and Literary Churchman) Thus, O faithful child of thy country, runs my letters to the *Literary Churchman*, therefore I beg thee, **be earnest for their publication**, that thou mayst obtain a copy, and compare it with the copy in thy hands. And if it be incorrectly translated, and then published, let me know, or else do thou publish the real text of my letter in Greek, and send me a copy of the journal; but let it be quickly, for in the new year (God willing) **I shall go to Jerusalem and thence to Damascus, because the Roman Catholics and the followers of Mohammed have some evil scheme against us.** But I will write to thee again from Jerusalem, and send thee the copy of the inscriptions from Bostrae, and Syria, and Palestine. Farewell again and many times, my son in the Lord,

and fight the good fight, and write to thy Spiritual Father.
+ Kallinikos Hieromonachos

Alexandria, 6 November, 1862.

Kallinikos FIVE. 3 December, 1862: *The Guardian* **(Written before lettes thee and four above. A separate and similar letter, bearing the same post mark: Alexandria, 16**[th] **October, 1862 appeared in** *The Literary Churchman* **of 16**[th] **December 1862. Both contain the Greek with an English translation. The following from the** *English Churchman* **is somewhat longer. Written from Alexandria**

.....**You are aware of all that the excellent and much enduring Simonides has published as to the Pseudo Sinaitic Codex, abstracted from the library of the Greek monastery at Sinai, by Dr. Tischendorf. The facts are really so.** And I counsel you not to continue circulating contrary statements, for you will greatly sin in foisting on the world a new MS. as an old one, and especially a MS. containing the Holy Scriptures. Injury to the Church must accrue from all this, even from the evidently numerous corrections of the MS. And that this is a new MS. I openly proclaim, both before the all - seeing God, and before men; and further I protest to you, Messrs. Editors, that this is a genuine work of the indefatigable Simonides. For **I myself saw him with my own eyes, in February, <u>1840</u>, writing it in Athos**; and, owing to the death of the head of the monastery, he left the work unfinished, and went to **Constantinople**, taking the Codex with him, which also he delivered to the illustrious patriarch **Constantius**, and he sent it to the monastery in **Sinai** by a monk of that house, named **Germanus, whose subordinate still lives in Athos** to attest the writer. **And the partiarch sent the Codex there, in order that the transcript might be compared with other copies of the Old and New Testament, and then be transcribed by the same Simonides, and sacredly presented to the Emperor of Russia**, on the part, not of the monastery of St. Pantaleemon, according to the original intention of Benedict, but on the part of the patriarch Constantius. On this account, the hieromonk **Callistratus**, a wise man, and companion of the same house, undertook the comparison of it, and **did compare it with other codices** of the same house, by command of Constantius, the patriarch. And he, **having partly corrected it, left it in the library awaiting the return of Simonides, the first calligrapher in Greece**. He not coming in good time, the work was altogether neglected, and **remained in the common library of the monastery for some time: until Dr. Tischendorf (coming to the monastery in Sinai, in <u>May, 1844</u>**, and spending some days there, and having examined the MS. carefully and suspecting it to be ancient), **tore off a small part of it privately, and went his way**, as if nothing had happened, leaving the rest of it in the position which it

CHAPTER 4: A THREEFOLD WITNESS AGAINST ANTIQUITY

had before. He perpetrated this great wrong without scruple. **Finally, coming again to the same monastery, he took also the remaining portion of the MS. with the aid of the Russian Consul, on the promise that he would return it.** And they both promised to the Bishop of Sinai many and great gifts, which, in my opinion, they will never perform: because, at other times, many such promises were made by a certain Russian archimandrite, named **Porphyrius**, who took away many MSS. from **the monastery of St. Dionysius, in Athos**, and from others, and they were never fulfilled.

All these things, then, I know, being on the spot, and 1 declare them openly for the dear truth's sake. **And I further assert, that the Codex** which, *per fas et nefas* **Dr. Tischendorf abstracted, is the very same which Simonides wrote <u>twenty - two years ago</u>. For I saw it in the hands of Tischendorf, and recognised the work, and I first mentioned it to Simonides, who had no knowledge of the fact before.** Evidently he knew not the abstraction of his work from the monastery in Mount Sinai. I read also at first this acrostic in it, «Simonides'entire work»: but, after two days, **the leaf containing this formal acrostic had been removed** - it being unknown, as yet, by whom this was done. I know too, still further, that **the same Codex was cleaned, with a solution of herbs, on the theory that the skins might be cleaned, but, in fact, that the writing might be changed, as it was, to a sort of yellow colour**.

These things then, Messrs. Editors, I have thought it my duty, unasked, to make known to you before I die -for I am an old man, and very near to death; and you, being as you are, heralds of the truth- as such you will greatly serve the truth, and those who follow truth, if you will exactly publish the contents of this my letter; or, otherwise, you will give account to

God in the Day of Judgment. Farewell in the Lord, &c. Your very devoted servant, and earnest worshipper of God,

CALLINICUS HIEROMONK Alexandria, October 16—28, 1862. (Elliott pp. 76,77).

Kallinikos SIX. 2 November 1863: *The Literary Churchman*

Greeting in the Lord. On my arrival in the island of Rhodes, from Beyrout, I found in circulation **many absurd and ridiculous stories (for which I was not prepared) attacking the genuineness of my letter which I sent to you from Alexandria. I pity those who have published falsehoods so unfounded**; for it appears to me, that these men attempt to mislead public opinion for the sake of individual interest; but I understand that «the golden fountains are babblings as the proverb says.

And so I say to you boldly, for the sake of sacred truth, that I sent three letters from Alexandria, one to the Editor of the *Guardian*, a second to the *Times*, and a third to the *Literary Churchman*. I wrote them myself, **my subordinate, Eusebius, copied them**, and then I signed and forwarded them, and sent the original to Simonides; and they who say the contrary, utter a manifest falsehood, for Simonides had no previous knowledge about these letters, but when he found from me what I had done, reproved me for it properly, because he did not wish the matter to be borne testimony to by me, for political reasons.

And further, **I repeat, that the MS. in dispute is the work of the unwearied Simonides, and of no other person. A portion of this was secretly removed from Mt. Sinai, by Professor Tischendorf, in 1844.**

CHAPTER 4: A THREEFOLD WITNESS AGAINST ANTIQUITY

The rest, with inconceivable recklessness, he mutilated and tampered with, according to his liking, in the year 1859. Some leaves he destroyed, especially such as contained the Acrostics of Simonides; but four of them escaped him, viz., one in the Old Testament, and three in Hermas, as I long since informed Simonides: many palaeographical symbols also escaped his notice, but I do not know whether these were eventually overlooked.

I have to add, that some of **the more foolish among our monks at Cairo were bribed to copy and sign certain letters sent from Leipzig and England, containing many things adverse to Simonides.** I do not know, for certain, what came of it; but I warn you not to fall into the modes of those who are systematically plotting against humanity for the sake of lifeless gold. Farewell, Pardon the old man, Kallinikos Hieromonachos Rhodes, Sept. 17, 1863. (Elliott pp. 113,114).

Kallinikos SEVEN. 11th November 1863: *The Guardian*

+ To the Editor of the Guardian, greeting Joy unto thee,

I am astonished that they are not ashamed who give out that Simonides wrote the letter which I addressed to thee last year from Alexandria, concerning the MS. taken away from Mount Sinai by Professor Tischendorf.

I, friend Editor, wrote that letter of my own accord and through the medium of my clerk, Eusebius, and I signed it with my own hand; and this I did for truth's sake, and that I might free humanity from Tischendorf's error. I also wrote two more letters on the same subject, and besides these I wrote also others to Simonides on the same subject.

And as regards the letters, I wrote them all. But Simonides wrote the Codex that was taken by Tischendorf from Mount Sinai, and which was corrupted by Tischendorf himself. Let therefore those give over that distort truth for the sake of worldly interest.

Know also that lately **two pseudo—monks have been hired** that they may write against Simonides and make their nonsense known through the English press, as at other times also those miserable men did in Germany, France and Turkey.

Good health unto thee in the Lord, and excuse

+ Callinikus the Monk who blesseth thee with all his heart. (Elliott pp. 114,115).

C. WHAT J.E. HODGKIN OF LIVERPOOL SAID

Constantine Simonides had a firm friend and supporter in J. Eliot Hodgkin of Liverpool. Hodgkin was more than a match for W. Aldis Wright and answered well the arguments levelled against Simonides. He became the recipient of the letters that Kallinkos wrote to Simonides and defended their validity. His archive of these letters is at the British Library in London. It was Hodgkin's view that the *Greek* Simonides had been treated unfairly and in an "un-English" manner.

CHAPTER 4: A THREEFOLD WITNESS AGAINST ANTIQUITY

http://www.artinliverpool.com/liverpools-museum-the-first-150-years/

World Museum Liverpool 1860

Given Hodgkin's importance in this debate, it says something of the bias of J.K. Elliott that he tells us nothing about the man or his credentials. There certainly is no similar omission for those attacking Simonides. Hodgkin was curator of the Mayer Museum in Liverpool. It contained collections of many thousands of drawings, engravings, and autograph letters relating to the history of art in England. It also was renowned for its large and growing collection of Egyptian antiquities. The Mayer collections became a major part of the new Museum that was constructed in 1860. Hodgkin and Simonides had shared interests previously and with his support Simonides had a very substantial ally. By so openly giving his support Hodgkin put his own reputation on the line.

Hodgkin ONE. 14 January 1863: *The Guardian*

Sir—**The originals of the four letters from Kallinikos**, which Simonides forwards to you for publication, are in my possession, as he has handed them to me, to preserve for the inspection of any gentleman who may incline to examine them. **I have myself given them very minute examination**, and, as far as my experience in such matters goes, **I have no hesitation in pronouncing them to be the genuine productions of some one person**, and to have been written at the respective dates assigned to them. Three of them bear postmarks corresponding with the MS. dates; the fourth has been transmitted in an envelope. The handwriting is very much cramped and contracted, so as to be in places almost illegible, but I think you may rely on the translation as literal and accurate.

In conclusion I wish distinctly to remark that I simply hold these letters for the inspection of the curious in such matters, and of those interested in the question of the authenticity of the «Codex Sinaiticus», and that whilst I have given my closest and most minute attention to the examination of the external appearance, I do not wish to be understood as taking any part in the controversy **but would request those who have ridiculed the statements of Simonides to come and inspect for themselves these**

CHAPTER 4: A THREEFOLD WITNESS AGAINST ANTIQUITY

documents, which form, I imagine, if they are what they profess to be, an important link in the evidence. John Eliot Hodgkin   Liverpool, Jan. 3, 1863 (Elliott 91,92).

Hodgkin TWO. 14 January 1863: *The Guardian* (second letter, published on same date)

Sir—Facts are stubborn things, and one simple fact, which 1 happen to be in a position to establish, knocks down the beautiful theory of fraud and falsehood at the hands of Simonides which your correspondent Mr. W.A.Wright has so generously sought to establish in his letter to you of December 10 which 1 have seen to - day for the first time. Mr. Wright «has reason to believe that Simonides first became aware of the existence of the Codex Friderico – Augustanus [the initial name Tischendorf gave to Codex Sinaiticus] on the 7th of October of the present year (1862)», and thereupon goes into arguments to prove that Simonides (whom he assumes, with a candour worthy of the rest of his letter, to be one with Kallinikos) had time to transmit this «newly acquired fact» to Alexandria, and for it to be returned, &c. Alas for Mr. W.A. Wright and his «reasons to believe». Simonides first saw the facsimilies of the Codex Friderico - Augustanus at my house in the spring of 1861 - some twenty months before the date so kindly set down for his first view by your correspondent. It is only the accident of my being acquainted with the fact that Simonides had seen and studied the Codex at that period which rescues him from the maliciously ingenious reasoning of Mr. Wright. So much for that gentleman, his reasons, and his conclusions. Ex pede Herculem.

I am no «thick - and - thin» partisan of Simonides. I should expose any fraud of his which I might detect with as unsparing a hand as Mr. Wright himself; but I will not see the public misled by such unscrupulous special pleading as that of your correspondent without calling attention to the fallacy, and to the animus which prompts it. John Eliot Hodgin West Derby, Jan. 3, 1863. (Elliott 92).

Hodgkin THREE. 28 January 1863: *The Journal of Sacred Literatuee*

…..It is now just three years since Simonides first committed to writing in England (in a letter to Mr. Charles Stewart, dated 4th Jan., 1860) his version of the Codex Sinaiticus. He had his own reasons, I suppose, for not letting the whole public into the secret at an earlier period than last autumn, but the facts of his early claim are well known to his friends. **It was not till he saw in Mr. Newton's hands the facsimile of the Codex Sinaiticus, published by Tischendorf, that he felt as perfectly assured as he has since done that the MS. was his own work** (Elliott p.39)…..

Hodgkin FOUR. 28January 1863: *The Guardian*

Sir—At the risk of again «amusing» you, I venture to suggest that you have hardly appreciated at its true value the bearing of the letters which you have published in your last impression.

Permit me very briefly to recall to your recollection the facts. **A letter vouching for the truth of the narrative of Simonides reached you from Alexandria. Correspondents hostile to Simonides at once suggested that the professed author of that letter, Kallinikos, was no other than Simonides himself in disguise**, and ingenious calculations were entered into to prove that there had been time for him, since he had been put upon his trial in England, to send out instructions to Egypt, and to have the forged voucher for his veracity returned to you. On the face of it, one would say that such a device, if resorted to, was the sudden and improvised expedient of an almost desperate man.

But at this point of the controversy turn up no less than four letters from the same Kallinikos (bearing the same signature, at any rate, as the recent letter to the *Literary Churchman*, as I can testify myself), written various dates from the year 1858 to 1861and giving evidence by their post - marks of having been really posted at those dates. I submit that the fact of the existence of these letters, all certainly written by the same person. whoever he may be, and **especially of the letter dated August 5 (17). 1858. long before the publication of Tischendorf s statement** as to his discovery of the «Codex Sinaiticus» throws fresh light upon the whole question, and **should secure for the Hieromonachos a more respectful hearing than some of your correspondents are disposed to allow him.**

Whether my last letters to you were «lrish» in their character I will not now discuss. I can only say that **nothing but the English love of fair play first led me to inquire into the character and history of a man whom for years 1 knew of only as «the notorious Simonides», but whom subsequent investigation showed me to be oppressed by the unfair treatment of antagonists.**

To the same instinctive love of justice on your part I appeal, to give the facts recently brought forward whatever weight they really deserve; and repeating that I shall be most happy to exhibit the original letters to any reader of your paper, clerical or lay, who may favour me with a call here -1 am, yours truly,

John Eliot Hodgin West Derby, near Liverpool. (Elliott pp. 94,95).

Hodgkin FIVE. 18 February 1863: *The Guardian*

Sir - During the meeting last Wednesday of the Royal Society of Literature, **1 was called on, in a peremptory manner, by Mr. W.A. Wright, to exhibit the four letters signed «Kallinikos Hieromonachos» which were committed to my charge.** I declined to obey Mr. Wright, and offered to give my reasons for this course, which, however, the meeting did not seem to require. With your permission I will briefly state the most important of them, the others being of a personal nature connected with the character of a private, correspondence with me which Mr. W. A. Wright had commenced.

I considered, and still consider, the course adopted by the Royal Society of Literature, at their last meeting, to be a most unfair and un-English one. At a meeting ostensibly convened for the reception of a report of the council on the Mayer Papyri professedly unrolled by Simonides, which was sure to challenge a vigorous reply from those who held the arguments of that body to be weak and one - sided, it was attempted to preclude the healthy discussion of that report, by **the immediate introduction of a paper by Mr. W. A. Wright on the Codex Sinaiticus, the simple object of which appeared to be to shake the faith of the public in the personal character of Simonides.** A very strong clique attempted to rule that this paper should be read before the discussion on the Mayer Papyri could take place, but the desire of fair play was so strong among some of the neutral party that the meeting condescended to allow the report of the council to be discussed first, though the controversy was much curtailed by the eagerness of the friends of the Codex Sinaiticus, for the paper which was to throw discredit on the pretensions of Simonides. This paper was read, and personal evidence was called in support of it, which I believe I only speak

CHAPTER 4: A THREEFOLD WITNESS AGAINST ANTIQUITY

the feeling of the meeting in describing as extremely discreditable.

After the meeting, I had some conversation with Mr. W. A. Wright, the result of which was that I promised to examine still more minutely the handwriting. I have done this, and feel that the controversy has now reached a stage at which **it is best for me no longer to retain the guardianship of the four letters**, but to place them still more easily within the reach of those gentlemen who may wish to examine them. I send them, therefore, to the **Rev. W. J. Irons, D.D., Brompton**, who has kindly consented to take charge of them - not as editor of the Literary Churchman (in which character some one addressed him in error at the meeting on Wednesday), but because he has taken so great an interest in the matter during the illness of the editor of that journal, that he has a comprehensive view of the merits of the case.

I would beg those gentlemen who examine these letters, to give them their earnest and minute attention, and considering the great importance of the issue, to weigh calmly and seriously the various questions which may arise during their scrutiny. And I think that the judgment of some perfectly unbiased and competent expert should be obtained if possible. John Eliot Hodgkin. (Elliott pp. 99,100).

Hodgkin SIX. 22 July 1863: *The Guardian*

Sir— I wish to make a few remarks under the above well —worn heading, on a subject which deeply concerns myself—viz., my «champion-ship», as it is called, of Simonides. I shall be gladly indebted to your courtesy for the publication of my letter, which 1 will condense as much as possible.

One of my friends showed my yesterday an article in the Christian Remembrancer for July, headed Constantine Simonides and his Biblical Studies, containing two statements which 1 wish to correct, though made by a writer of whose tone as regards myself I have in order respects no cause to complain.

The first is unimportant, but may as well be set straight: I did not accompany Simonides to Cambridge last year, as is stated on p. 201; if I had done so, I should have been able to correct at the time Mr. W.A. Wright's idea that Simonides was up to that date unacquainted with the Codex Friderico - Augustanus.

The other statement of which I have to complain, as hardly giving a fair impression of my conduct, even though it may be literally correct, is the following, on p. 206— «This leaf [the 1958 letter of Kallinikos to Simonides], we are sorry to be obliged to add, Mr. Hodgkin at first declined to exhibit». It seems to be suggested that I had suspicions of the genuineness of this leaf, and withheld it, while producing its companions. The fact is, as I think I sufficiently explained in my letter to you of February 14 that on a certain evening, at a meeting of the Royal Society of Literature, I declined to produce, not that leaf only, but the whole of the four letters which were called for, I thought somewhat imperiously, by Mr. W.A. Wright. I admit that I was **annoyed at the scant civility shown to the defenders of the claims of Simonides by his opponents**, and I thought that the jury empanelled to try the cause showed signs of something like a foregone conclusion. Under these circumstances, **I did what was equivalent to moving a new trial**. I declined to produce the letters there and then, but placed them at once {vide my letter to you dated February 14) in responsible hands in London (the Rev. W.J. Irons. D.D. Brompton),

CHAPTER 4: A THREEFOLD WITNESS AGAINST ANTIQUITY

suggesting at the same time that not merely amateur investigation should be pursued, but that an expert should be employed to examine them.

I see that some gentleman who has looked at the letters has made the observation, which was patent to any close observer, that **the paper of the letters on the single leaf was folded before the letter was written**, but he has not carried his observation far enough, or he would have also discovered that the letter written on a whole sheet, not enclosed in an envelope, but bearing the proper post - marks, and which must have come in its present state from Alexandria, has also been written after **the paper was folded, in accordance, as I am informed by a Greek gentleman, with the common practice in the East**. This fact, coupled with the circumstances that **all the letters are in the same handwriting**, warranted my original assertion, that they appeared to be «the genuine productions of one person, and written at the dates assigned to them». I do not press this view now, as the subject has become much more involved and difficult since I thus wrote, but it is necessary that I should show that I acted, not only with good faith, but after an examination even more minute than that of subsequent observers. One single circumstance I have noticed, since the meeting, in connection with these letters, to which no one has called attention, which I cannot explain by any theory, and which time alone can clear up. I will fully allude to it when I obtain the information referred to below.

And now you must allow me, once for all, to put myself right with the literary public as to the nature of my «defence» of Simonides. It has been an occupation unsought by and not congenial to me, sometimes even irksome; but whatever I have done, **I have felt it my duty to do—a duty, in the first instance, to one who**

was thrown in my path, assailed on all sides, apparently innocent of the charges brought against him, a foreigner and nearly friendless, and who could not understand but through a medium of his own language, a quarter of the statements adverse to his pretensions with which the papers teemed. The feelings, however, **which now mainly urge me to do my part towards obtaining him a fair hearing** in the many causes in which he has contrived to get himself arraigned at the bar of public opinion are the persuasion that his pretensions have at any rate too much plausibility and show of truth to be silenced by declamation, and the assurance that full discussion will soonest elicit the truth. If Simonides have (sic) spoken falsely, he will in the end most assuredly convict himself, and Mr. W.A. Wright and I, if we are engaged in eliciting facts and not mere theories, are not antagonists, but are working towards one end — truth. My action has hitherto been principally confined to stating such facts as I could really vouch for, and to putting Simonides as far as I could in the position he would have held could he have understood our language. **But I believe that I possess clues which, properly followed up, may lead to the entire removal of many of our doubts.** Perhaps it is too much to expect that we shall ever really get at the whole truth on both sides. I am now waiting information from the East from sources unknown to Simonides, which should produce a definite result; and any reliable statements shall be made public as early as possible. If it turns out that the assertion made by Simonides that he wrote the Codex Sinaiticus, wild though it seems, is correct, I shall be glad that I have done my part towards the development of the inquiry; yet I shall do my best towards testing the truth of his every declaration. And there is not a man in England who will have more right or more inclination than myself to unite in the chorus of indignation which will for ever pursue him, should he be eventually proved, after all his protestation, to be guilty of the imposture of which he is now virtually accussed.

John Eliot Hodgkin. (Elliott pp. 95-97).

Hodgkin SEVEN. 26th August, 1863: *The Guardian*

....May I ask you to use your exertions to obtain from Tischendorf a minute account of his successive discoveries of the two portions of this MS. **Am I mistaken in saying that no details of discoveries whatever were offered with the Codex Friderico-Augustanus, at the time of publication.** And is not a much more connected and detailed account to be looked for than has yet been published (in English, at least) of the various stages in the discovery and deportation of the remainder of the volume?

....It is somewhat remarkable that when inquiries were made in February, 1861, at Mount Sinai, by the Rev. W. W. Woollcomb, of Salford, about the Biblical MS. sent thence by Tischendorf to the Emperor, **the reply of the librarian was «that he knew nothing about the matter, that he never heard of any MS. being sent to the Emperor, or brought away by Tischendorf »**. (Elliott p.16)....

Hodgkin EIGHT. 1 September 1863: *The Literary Churchman*

Dear Sir, - The accompanying letter is an accurate copy of that written by Simonides, on the 4 -16 Jan., 1860, to Mr. Charles Steuart, of Brighton, claiming the «Codex Sinaiticus» as his own performance. I deeply regret that an accurate translation of this letter did not appear at an early stage of the controversy.....

I am, Dear Sir, yours truly, J. Eliot Hodgkin. (Elliott p. 40).

Hodgkin NINE. 2 December, 1863: *The Guardian* (summarised in *The Literary Churchman*)

SIMONIDES AND BENEDICT

Sir-You assume that the letter from Mr. Wilkinson, published in the Guardian of November 11, will annihilate Simonides.... I submit that, on the contrary, it only affords evidence that any statement, no matter how loose, is readily adopted, if it impugns the veracity of so troublesome a correspondent as the former; and when I have shown, as I shall presently do, that the most important assertions of the Archimandrite Dionysius are false, I imagine that his letter will damage instead of aiding the cause of the opponents of Simonides. I shall first reply to those assertions of Dionysius which can be most readily disproved, and then give the rejoinder of Simonides to the rest.

In reply to Mr. W.A. Wright's second question, Dionysius says that Benedict died indeed in 1840, but in April, not in August. In a letter written to the Editor of the *Telegraph of the Bosphorus*, and published in that journal in December, 1851, a bitter opponent of Simonides, Melchisedec, on the Monastery of Laura, states that the death of Benedict took place in May.

In reply to the third question, Dionysius states that Simonides was neither the nephew of Benedict, nor was he in any way related to him. I have before me the *Telegraph of the Bosphorus* of the 8th of December, 1851, in which is the commencement of the article above alluded to, written by one who has spared no pains in casting discredit upon the pretensions of Simonides to the discovery of **the secret library in the Rossico**

CHAPTER 4: A THREEFOLD WITNESS AGAINST ANTIQUITY

monastery. Yet in this article Benedict is spoken of in the highest terms, and always as the uncle of Simonides. Had there been the smallest doubt about the relationship existing between them, the fact would have been eagerly seized on in this hostile letter of Melchisedec.

I can in the same manner entirely disprove the implied assertion of Dionysius, that Simonides was only at Mount Athos during a part of the year 1840, and that, too, curiously enough, by the testimony of another opponent, hailing from the same monastery as your informant Dionysius.

In the same number of the *Telegraph of the Bosphorus* is a diatribe against Simonides, by a correspondent signing himself «E. Xeropotamenos», in which occurs this passage - «I have only to add that Simonides remained in the Holy Mountain two years, from 1838 to 1841; but where he got a knowledge of palaeography I could not discover».

This writer has given Simonides a still longer stay than he himself claims, and thus entirely refutes the implied negative given by Dionysius to Mr. W.A. Wright's query....I conceive that the replies I have thus given, on the authority of adversaries of Simonides, will be taken as pretty **conclusively settling Mr. W.A. Wright's questions Nos. 3 and 5, and as showing that even in the question** of the month in which Benedict died the objectors are at variance.

Whilst the opponents of Simonides are continually accusing him of inconsistency and inaccuracy, they seem to forget how many contradictions have already crept into the charges against him. I subjoin three statements, all made by hostile writers, which will confirm what I have just stated:

Nicolaides says, (*Parthenon*, Feb. 28, 1863) - «I am well acquainted with all the monasteries of Mount Athos.... I never heard of the monk Benedictus, and do not believe he ever existed».

Dionysius says (*Guardian*, Nov. 1, 1863) - «Benedict belonged to the Russian monastery, but he was never the spiritual head of the monks».

Melchisedec of Laura says (*Telegraph of Bosphorus*, Dec. 8, 1861) - «That Benedict was distinguished both as a scholar and as a wise man, all those who knew his character admit».

The fact that one informant, who says he is well acquainted with all the monasteries in Mount Athos, is entirely ignorant of the existence of so important a character as Benedict, should make us pause before accepting as readily as you seem inclined to do the last set of imputations on the veracity of Simonides.

I will now condense the explanations given by Simonides himself of the motives which led Dionysius to make the statements which have appeared.

Between the two classes of monastery in Mount Athos, the Coenobiac and the Idiorhythmic, there is the greatest rivalry, and in many cases even enmity. The monks of the former class consider that those of the latter have obtained funds which were originally intended for their own order, and that these funds, derived from possessions in Moldavia, Wallachia, &c, are moreover grossly misapplied in detail. Whatever may be the merits of this controversy, which has long existed, one thing is certain, that **Simonides, in his zeal for the Rossico and other Coenobiac monasteries**, has for many years | spoken openly and bitterly against some

CHAPTER 4: A THREEFOLD WITNESS AGAINST ANTIQUITY

of the principal men of the Idiorhythmic, of whom he has, of course, made deadly enemies.

Such were his antagonists already cited, Melchisedec of Laura and Efugenius) of Zeropotami; such is this present accuser Dionysious of Zeropotami. A reference to pp. 116, 117, 139 of the book concerning Nicolas, Bishop of Methone, published by Simonides in London in 1858, will show that he attacks the above trio by name.

It is strange that Mr. Wilkinson, instead of writing to the head of the Rossico monastery, was ^obliged to apply» to the head of a monastery of the other order, and to a man well known to be opposed to Simonides. This may be the way to get rid of this troublesome gentleman, but it is not the way to get at the whole truth.

Simonides further says that Benedict was the spiritual head of the monastery, though during the last few years of his life he retired from the secular duties connected with his position. He refers you to the Patriarch of Constantinople for confirmation of the truth of this statement.

I hope to be able to discover from some of the Greek newspapers, what was the position of Benedict at the close of his life; the part which he took in the re-establishment of the Rossico monastery was one of the points in dispute between Simonides and Melchisedec.

Simonides repeats that he died in August. The question may not be an important one, but, as his opponents disagree, we may allow that the nephew is probably in the right.

In reply to question No. 4, he says that as the discovery was kept utterly secret at the time, it is impossible for any person to declare that it was or was not made, except those actually engaged in it.

It is clear that Dionysius did not understand the bearing of No. 5, as his reply is wide of the mark.

Dionysius [different from the above Dionysius] **is, or was, a celebrated calligrapher in the Rossico monastery**: he was originally a private monk of the οκετε of St. Anna; he copied the treatise of Pauselenus about Dionysius of Agrapha at the request of Pappa Macarius for M. Didron. It is possible that he is mentioned in that work.

I have extremely condensed the statements of Simonides, but will obtain full answers to other points connected with the queries, if it be desired. (Elliott pp.73-75)....

A chronological and uninterrupted reading of the letters of Simonides, Kalinikos, and Hodgkin and noting particularly the emboldened statements can quite naturally lead to the conclusion that the truth was being told. Under a welter of hostile reaction this testimony remained compelling and consistent. The fact that the academia of that day concluded that Sinaiticus was old does not diminish the force of the opposing argument any more than the creationist's argument is diminished by the general acceptance of evolution. We can be thankful that the debate is being revived and the assumed antiquity of Sinaiticus is increasingly being placed under the spotlight; and (!), the implications this has for Vaticanus.

CHAPTER 5
A SURGE OF VATICAN "INTEREST" IN TISCHENDORF AND SINAITICUS

Mount Athos, Saint Catherine in Sinai, Simonides and Kalinikos, Tsar Nicolas are of course Greek Orthodox. They represent, with Roman Catholicism on the other side, the great historic divide in Europe. There has never been much love lost between them. The letters of Simonides and Kalinikos do not show a great deal of anti-Romanism but they do remind us who they are with respect to this divide.

Kalinikos Letter TWO: Farewell, O son in the Lord, and fight the good fight, and write to me sometimes, that we may hear of thy good deeds in behalf of our nation, and **our mother the Church**, from their author, the faithful son of his country, and not from others.

Kalinikos Letter FOUR: **I shall go to Jerusalem and thence to Damascus, because the Roman Catholics and the followers of Mohammed have some evil scheme against us.**

With the Reformation and Bibles based on the Received Text flooding Europe it is no mystery or surprise that Rome would seek to undermine what they called the *PAPER POPES* of the Protestants. James White in his debate with Chris Pinto is miles off when he belittles the idea of "Jesuit conspiracy" and Catholic involvement in the textual debate. https://www.youtube.com/watch?v=nzRTuUJugSY

Bill Cooper's book devotes a great deal to what should be an obvious fact to anyone studying the history of the Reformation Bibles – Vatican opposition and involvement against the spread of Scripture and Bibles based on the Received Text. Moreover, Cooper documents that when Tischendorf came to the Sinai monastery and made trips across Europe promoting his "discovery" *he was being courted by Rome*! Thus whatever may be the difficulty in this story to connect all the dots, this is a fact that is beyond dispute. We have already noted (Chapter III; Elliott pp. 10-12) Tischendorf's warmth toward the Vatican and delight at Cardinal Mai's publication of Codex Vaticanus on **Easter 1858**, and then his upmost joy at being shown at Sinai the remaining sections of Sinaiticus in **1859** (having failed to receive any help from the monks in **1853**). (Elliott p. 10).

> You know **what weight the learned world attaches to the famous Vatican MS. of the Bible, and how it has for centuries been esteemed one of the special treasures of the Papal library**: you are aware how anxious men have been, and how difficult they have found it, to collate even single passages, **how earnestly Mai's edition, undertaken by order of the Pope, had been looked for since 1828, and how gladly it was at last received, at Easter 1858**, after thirty years delay. (Elliott p. 10).

As the man who could and would make the most of the Sinaiticus manuscript, we must ask if Tischendorf was

CHAPTER 5: A SURGE OF VATICAN "INTEREST"

"steered" by Rome to his discovery of its remaining contents so soon after the publication of Vaticanus. Certainly he was "feted" by Rome in the previous years. Such a scenario involves contradictions, yet that is how conspiracy works. The evidence for such a scenario is overwhelming.

Tischendorf was a Lutheran and his patron overseeing his 1959 visit to the Sinai monastery (Greek Orthodox) was the Emperor Alexander II of Russia (Russian Orthodox). For Rome to "steer" Tischendorf to Sinaiticus in 1859 and avoid suspicion would seem to be difficult. Yet, we note that this time the monks at the monastery were helpful, whereas six years before they were not. And, significantly, (very significantly!), in the years before there was a major factor in place that meant that Tischendorf would be "steered" by Rome. When, Tischendorf, a Lutheran, "discovered" the *amazing* codex at Sinai in **1844** he did not give it a Lutheran name. He called it **Codex Friderico - Augustanus.**

Frederick Augustus II was king of Saxony from 1833 until his death in an accident in 1854. Saxony (bordering Poland and the Czech Republic) was largely Protestant but its kings were Catholic, and with so much of Europe now Protestant, that fact made these kings a special favourites of Rome. King Frederick was the chief benefactor to Tischendorf in his travels (he paid the bills for his travel). That gave Rome an opportunity to direct events then, and influence the course of events even after Frederick's untimely death.

WAS CODEX SINAITICUS WRITTEN IN 1840!

https://cdn.britannica.com/300x200/30/11730-004-5EAA6014.jpg

King Frederick Augustus II, Rome's Benefactor to Tischendorf

(1) TISCHENDORF'S COURTSHIP WITH THE VATICAN

Cooper (p. 15) has provided us with an astounding quotation from Tischendorf. It demonstrates the utter adulation that Catholicism was heaping on Tischendorf and Tischendorf's utter willingness to receive and revel in it.

I had been commended in the most earnest manner by Guizot to the French Ambassador, Count Latour Maubourg; I was also favored with many letters of introduction from Prince John of Saxony to his personal friends of high rank; and in addition with a very flattering note from the Archbishop Affre, of Paris, directed to **[Pope] Gregory XVI., The latter, after a**

CHAPTER 5: A SURGE OF VATICAN "INTEREST"

prolonged audience granted to me, took an ardent interest in my undertaking; Cardinal Mai received me with kind recognition; [and] Cardinal Mezzofanti honored me with some Greek verses composed in my praise... (George Merrill, *The Parchments and the Faith*, p. 176, citing *Leipziger Zeitung* for 31 May 1866).

Observing the *BIG THREE* mentioned above, the Jesuit, **Cardinal Mezzofanti** was Custodian of the Vatican Library. In 1843, the year before his Sinai "discovery", Tischendorf was given an audience with **Pope Gregory** and allowed the first view by a Protestant of Codex Vaticanus. This according to Cooper was in spite of a "well-rehearsed show of horrified objection" by **Cardinal Mai** who was preparing the facsimile of Vaticanus (p. 22).

Note also that that in the midst of this flurry of Vatican activity that Tischendorf met with the Pope one year before the Pope issued his decree against Bible Societies (8 May 1844).

(2) AN INCENTIVE FOR A VATICAN PLOT: POPES CANNOT PERFORM APOSTOLIC MIRACLES

There is a strange and unique similarity between Codex Sinaiticus and Codex Vaticanus. Apart from a 12th Century manuscript located in Paris (304) these are the only two Greek manuscripts that omit Mark 16:9-20. This fact, however, takes a bizarre turn when we discover that the "replacement" pages leading up to and "clumsily" designed to divert attention from the omitted section *were written in both manuscripts by the same scribe*.

It was Tischendorf himself who was the first to recognize this same hand at work. But now we are really on a "roller coaster" and cannot stop there. Tischendorf then came to the further and astounding conclusion that the scribe who wrote in these two "lead-up sections" also wrote the entire New Testament portion of Codex Vaticanus. This is not new information, it is well documented from the time (Hort and others recognized it), but considered now in the light of Sinaiticus being a recent production, it has huge implications. It points undeniably to Vatican involvement in both manuscripts.

If the Popes are the true successors to the Apostles, they according to the Lord's promises in Mark 16:9-20 would be able to perform these *signs of an apostles* (2 Cor. 12:12; Acts 5:16). THEY CANNOT! In fact the Apostles themselves would *not* be able to perform these miracles (as the emphasis of Mark 16 shows) unless *they started believing*! Thankfully, they did start believing.

> *16:9 Now when Jesus was risen early the first day of the week, he appeared first to Mary Magdalene, out of whom he had cast seven devils. 10 And she went and told them that had been with him, as **they mourned and wept**. 11 And they, when they had heard that he was alive, and had been seen of her, **believed not**. 12 After that he appeared in another form unto two of them, as they walked, and went into the country. 13 And they went and told it unto the residue: **neither believed they them**. 14 Afterward he appeared unto the eleven as they sat at meat, and **upbraided them with their unbelief and hardness of heart, because they believed not** them which had seen him after he was risen. 15 And he said unto them, Go ye into all the world, and preach the gospel to every creature. 16 He that believeth and is baptized shall be saved; but he that believeth not*

*shall be damned. 17 And **these signs shall follow them that believe**; In my name shall they cast out devils; they shall speak with new tongues; 18 They shall take up serpents; and if they drink any deadly thing, it shall not hurt them; they shall lay hands on the sick, and they shall recover. 19 So then after the Lord had spoken unto them, he was received up into heaven, and sat on the right hand of God. 20 And they went forth, and preached every where, **the Lord working with them, and confirming the word with signs following. Amen**.*

As no signs like these ever followed a Pope, there is every likelihood that the Vatican conspired to remove Mark 16:9-20 from the Bible!

(3) ROME AND CODEX VATICANUS

Currently, the Old Testament of Vaticanus consists of 617 sheets and the New Testament of 142 sheets. Hebrews 9:14 through Revelation are missing and replaced by a 15th century minuscule supplement. Nothing was known about this famous and hugely defective manuscript at the Vatican before its mention in the library catalogues for the years 1475 and 1481. In the former it is merely given a shelf number (1209) and in the latter it is described as a *"Biblia* in three columns on vellum".

Its original writing cannot be seen as it has been re-inked and over-written. Cooper says this was done by a "15th century hand" (p. 23). According to *The Westminster Dictionary of the Bible*, ".....there is no prominent Biblical (manuscript) in which there occur such gross cases of misspelling, faulty grammar, and omission, as in Vaticanus." With Sinaiticus and *Papyri* [66,75] it contains the heretical *only begotten god* statement in John 1:18.

But note, Vaticanus has no history or provenance of how it came to the Vatican. There is no record of it ever being seen or heard of before its entry into the 1475 catalogue. The Vatican Library's earliest catalogue is 1475. A strange coincidence! It is not too much to ask if Vaticanus and the catalogue were produced in conjunction with each other.

Even Westcott and Hort acknowledged a Roman connection to Vatacanus. After pointing out that proper names are spelt as in the Latin Vulgate they say:

> Taking all kinds of indications together, we are inclined to surmise that Vaticanus [B] and Sinaiticus [א] were both written in the West, probably at Rome....(*The New Testament in the Original Greek*, pp.244-247. See Cooper, p. 25).

And (!), in 2007 a companion to codex Vaticanus was donated to the Vatican Library. It was *Papyri 75*, the largest of the papyri fragments and where extant containing almost verbatim the corrupted passages of Vaticanus. Like Vaticanus (or Sinaiticus) it has only a *shadowy* provenance; a Jesuit priest, Louis Doutreleau, obtained it from a "seller" in Cairo in 1952!! See Cooper's *worth the price of his book* account (95-103).

(4) SOME KEY QUESTIONS ABOUT ROME'S INVOLVEMENT

1. Why was Rome so reticent to allow scholars view Codex Vaticanus? Was it also a "recent production" that they were planning to spring upon Europe? Where they afraid that as it had no provenance, no copies, no chain of custody,

CHAPTER 5: A SURGE OF VATICAN "INTEREST"

(having "suddenly appeared"), that it would be exposed as a fraud?

2. Why did Rome wait until 1857 to publish Vaticanus? Rome would have realized that as a stand-alone manuscript it would not be accepted by Protestant scholars until it had support from from a similar kind of manuscript. The unexpected arrival of *Codex Friderico - Augustanus* provided that opportunity.

3. If Rome "pulled strings" for a revised Greek NT, why did they not formerly accept the revised text until 1975. Was it to avoid suspicion? Was it because they did not want a rival to their own Bible, the Latin Vulgate? Note: Rome cares nothing for the Bible, not even its own Bible, unless it can be used to promote its own ends. What the Papal Church says holds precedence over what the Bible says. To maintain this principle, faith in the Bible must be undermined and destroyed, and toward this end Tischendorf was being courted directed by Rome.

4. Assuming that Rome launched a conspiracy to bring Sinaiticus on board with Vaticanus; when did it begin? There is nothing in the letters of Simonides, Kallinikos and Hodgkin that indicates that the manuscript copied by Simonides was anything other then what it claimed to be – a gift to the Tsar of Russia. Yet as we will see below, whatever further may have happened at Sinai, the problem began *at Athos*!

5. As Rome's hand can be seen on both manuscripts, the fall of Sinaiticus from its seat of "antiquity" leads naturally to the fall of Vaticanus.

CHAPTER 6.
FURTHER QUESTIONS, FACTS AND FORENSICS

(1) WHY WAS THE CODEX BROUGHT TO SINAI RATHER THAN GOING DIRECTLY TO THE TSAR?

From Simonides' key letter of 3 September 1862, note again the steps taken by the codex from its conception to its delivery to the Sinai monastery (instead of to the Tsar). Clearly the best way to understand this debate is to focus on the 3 September 1862 letter and then to build upon it with further details from the other letters, sources and forensic information.

Simonides Letter THREE: About the **end of the year 1839**, the venerable **Benedict, my uncle, spiritual head of the monastery of the holy martyr Panteleemon in Mount Athos**, wished to present to the **Emperor Nicholas I., of Russia**, some gift from the sacred mountain, in grateful acknowledgement of the presents which had from time to time been offered to the monastery of the martyr. Not possessing anything which he deemed acceptable, he consulted with the **herald Procopius** and **the Russian monk Paul**, and they decided upon **a copy of the Old and New Testaments, written according to the ancient form, in capital letters**, and on parchment. This together with the remains of the seven apostolic fathers-**Barnabas, Hennas, Clement Bishop of Rome, Ignatius, Polycarp, Papias, and Dionysius the Areopagite-they proposed should be bound in gold, and presented to the Emperor** by a common friend. **Dionysius, the professional calligrapher** of the monastery, was then begged to undertake the work, but he declined, saying that the task being exceedingly difficult, he would rather not do so. In consequence of this, **I myself determined to begin the work**, especially as my revered uncle seemed earnestly to wish it. **Having then examined the principal copies of the Holy Scriptures preserved at Mount Athos, I began to practise the principles of calligraphy, and the learned Benedict taking a copy of the Moscow edition of both Testaments** (published and presented to the Greeks by the **illustrious brothers Zosimas**), **collated it with the ancient ones**, and by this means **cleared it of many errors**, after which he gave it into my hands to transcribe. Having then received both the Testaments, freed from errors (the old spelling, however, remaining unaltered), being short of parchment, I selected from the library of the monastery, with Benedict's permission, a **very bulky volume, antiquely bound, and almost entirely blank, the parchment of which was remarkably clean**, and beautifully finished. This had been prepared apparently many centuries ago - probably by the writer or by the principal of the monastery, as it bore the inscription...(a Collection of Panegyrics), and also a short discourse, much injured by time.

I therefore took possession of this book, and prepared it by taking out the leaf containing the discourse, and by removing several others injured by time and moths, after which I began my task. First, **I copied out the Old and New Testaments, then the Epistle of Barnabas, the first part of the pastoral writings of Hermas** in capital letters (or uncial characters) in the style known in calligraphy as....(amphidexios). The trancription of the remaining Apostolic writings, however, I declined, because the

CHAPTER 6: FURTHER QUESTIONS

supply of parchment ran short, and the severe loss which I sustained in **the death of Benedict** induced me to **hand the work over at once to the bookbinders** of the monastery, for the purpose of replacing the original covers, made of wood and covered with leather, which I had removed for convenience - and when he had done so, I took it into my possession.

Some time after this, **having removed to Constantinople, I showed the work to the patriarchs Anthimus and Constantius**, and communicated to them the reason of the transcription. Constantius took it, and, having thoroughly examined it**, urged me to present it to the library of Sinai**, which I accordingly promised to do. **Constantius had previously been Bishop of Sinai**, and since his resignation of that office had again become Perpetual Bishop of that place.

Shortly after this, I was placed under the protection of the illustrious **Countess Etleng and her brother, A. S. Stourtzas**, by the co-operation of two patriarchs; but, before departing for Odessa, I went, over **to the island of Antigonus to visit Constantius**, and to **perform my promise of giving up the manuscript to the library of Mount Sinai**. The patriarch was, however, absent from home, and I, consequently, left the packet for **him** with a letter. On his return, he wrote me the following answer:

My dearly beloved Son in the Holy Spirit, Simonides; Grace be with you and peace from God. **I received with unfeigned satisfaction your truly valuable transcript of the Holy Scriptures- namely, the Old and New Testaments, together with the Epistle of St. Barnabas and the first part of the pastoral writings of Hernias, bound in one volume, which shall be placed in the library of Mount Sinai,**

according to your wish. But I exhort you earnestly (if ever by God's will you should **return to the sacred Mount Athos) to finish the work** as you originally designed it, and he will reward you. Be with me on the 3d of next month, that I may give you letters to the illustrious **A. S. Stourtzas**, to inform him of your talents and abilities, and to give you a few hints which may prove useful to the success of your plans. I sincerely trust that you were born for the honour of your country. Amen. Constantius, late of Constantinople. — an earnest worshipper in Christ. Island of Antigonus, **13th Aug. 1841**.

After I have received the above letter, I again went to visit the patriarch, who gave me the kindest and most paternal advice, with letters to Stourtzas after which **I returned to Constantinople, and from thence went to Odessa in November, 1841**.

Here from this key letter, the question must be asked as to why at Constantinople did the Patriarch Constantius want the codex to be sent to Sinai instead of to the Russian Tsar. Constantius had the strongest of links to the Sinai monastery for he had been the Archbishop there. Kallinikos in the following letters indicate that Constantius felt that Simonides needed to do more work on the manuscript and that manuscripts housed at Sinai could help toward this. Nevertheless a great deal more than that was to befall the codex at Sinai and it would never reach the Tsar.

Kallinikos rebuked Simonides for not bringing the project to a conclusion.

CHAPTER 6: FURTHER QUESTIONS

Kallinikos Letter ONE:.....**These also send thee greeting, the Deacon Hilarion, and thy friends Nicander and Niphon, who lent thee the Books of Esdras at the time when thou wast preparing in Athos, at the exhoration of my uncle, the present (of the Holy Scriptures) to the glorious Emperor Nicholas**. They also wished to know whether the work was finished, and given to the Emperor, and whether thou wert suitably required for it; because they had no certain knowledge about these matters. **I told them all about it, and how the manuscript in question is now in Mount Sinai, and how thy indifference (forgive me, my son, for this true statement of mine) frustrated the original intention.** I certified them that this MS. of the Scriptures is still preserved in Sinai (as thou also knowest), because **I saw it there with my own eyes when I was in the Monastery of St. Catherine in <u>1845 in the month of July</u>**,

Kallinikos agrees with Constantius that the manuscript should be checked further at Sinai before sending it to the Tsar:

Kallinikos Letter TWO: + Dear Son in the Lord, Simonides, Grace be to thee and peace from the Father, Son, and Holy Spirit, One God.

That master and pupil of all guile, and all wickedness, the German **Tischendorf**, has unexpectedly rushed into thy net: for having inspected in **the common library** (where it was found a short time ago, and where it was placed by thy spiritual father **Callistratus** when he went to Alexandria) the Codex which thou wrotest at Athos, **<u>some twenty—two years ago</u>**, as a present to the deceased Emperor of Russia, Nicholas I, at the request of thy wise and distinguished uncle **Benedict,** and subsequently going to Constantinople after his death **gavest unfinished to the blessed Patriarch Constantius, who sent it to Mount Sinai by the Monk Germanus** of Sinai, whom thou knowest, and which was afterwards given to the **Hieromonachus Callistratus to be compared with the three old Codices of the Sacred Scriptures** (which thou knowest, and which are kept in the treasury), and was then disregarded because **thou didst not make thy appearance at the proper time** in Mount Sinai to transcribe it according to the earnest wish of the Patriarch, **he has proclaimed it as genuine, and as the oldest of all the known Codices in Europe** of the Old and New Testaments......

Matters were to take a strange turn at the Sinai monastery, though likely it was there that the many corrections were noted in the margins. These move strongly back to the Traditional, Received Text.

(2) WHAT ABOUT THE CLAIM THAT SINAITICUS WAS LISTED IN AN ANCIENT CATALOGUE?

Elliott writes:

One detail that was given about the finding of Codex Friderico-Augustanus was that it was found in a rubbish basket. A letter published in ***The Guardian* on 27th May 1863** from the Revd. J. Silvester Davies one - time chaplain to the British Consul in Alexandria....quotes a monk of Sinai.....that according to the librarian of the monastery **the whole of Codex Sinaiticus had been in the library for many years and**

was marked in the ancient catalogues. While this letter was written with the intention of supporting Tischendorf's claim that Sinaiticus....is ancient, it did cause scholars to question Tischendorf's statement about the condition in which he found the manuscript. **Is it likely, they wondered, that a manuscript known in the library catalogue would have been jettisoned in the rubbish basket** (p. 16)?

It is needless to say that if such a catalogue entry existed, the defenders of Codex Sinaiticus would have found the means to make it public. They have not! This simple fact is condemning evidence against the antiquity of Sinaiticus. Note again from Simonides letter of 16 June 1863, his grounds for denying that there was an ancient catalogue at Sinai:

> **Simonides Letter THIRTEEN**: I emphatically deny that the Codex Sinaiticus was inscribed in the Ancient Catalogue, for the good reason that no ancient catalogue exists; there was none there whatever, till I made a catalogue, during my first visit, for the Patriarch of Constantinople, Constantius, who before was Archbishop of Mount Sinai.

(3) WERE THE LETTERS WRITTEN AROUND THE WORM HOLES OR DID THE WORM HOLES GO THROUGH THE LETTERS?

If a scribe avoided the worm holes on the vellum it would of course show that the time of the writing was more recent than the age of the vellum. If the worm hole went through the vellum, then it is the opposite, the writing is older than the vellum. With Sinaiticus it is the former, the scribe avoided the worm holes. Regarding his obtaining vellum for the project, Simonides wrote:

> **Simonides Letter THREE**:....being short of parchment, I selected from the library of the monastery, with Benedict's permission, a **very bulky volume, antiquely bound, and almost entirely blank, the parchment of which was remarkably clean, and beautifully finished**. This had been prepared apparently many centuries ago - probably by the writer or by the principal of the monastery, as it bore the inscription...(a Collection of Panegyrics), and also a short discourse, much injured by time.
>
> I therefore took possession of this book, and prepared it by taking out the leaf containing the discourse, and by removing several others injured by time and moths, after which I began my task.

Cooper (pp. 32-34) gives examples and photographs of the scribe avoiding worm holes and other blemishes on the parchment. He also gives examples of deliberate tampering of the text; for example removal of or changes to words by so-called "worm" and "water" damage. The proof that this was deliberate was that only the place in question was affected and not the adjacent leaves.

(4) UNBOUND, DARKENED, FADED AT SINAI: THE COMPLICITYOF TISCHENDORF AND EVASIVENESS OF THE MONKS

According to Simonides the Codex that left Mt. Athos in 1841 or 42 and at least in appearance (if not in text) was

CHAPTER 6: FURTHER QUESTIONS

such as one would expect it to be as a gift to the Tsar of Russia. *It was fit for a king*! It was securely and attractively bound with clear and sharp lettering on the white vellum. Yet, as we saw above, at Constantinople, Constantius the former Archbishop of Sinai urged that it be "checked further" at Sinai before it was given to the Tsar. It never reached the Tsar! Simonides saw it ten years later at the Sinai monastery in an altogether different state. It was a dishevelled mess! From the white vellum and attractive single binding. It was disarranged and darkened at Sinai.

Today it is four sections of varying sizes in different parts of the world. Some of the pages are still white but most are "darkened". The locations of the four sections are -

- At the British Library (quire 34 [folio 8]; quires 37-46; 57-93). This is by far the largest.

- At Leipzig University (quires 35-37; 47-49).

- At the National Library of Russia (quires 3 [folio 4]; 11 [folio 2]; 38 [folio 8]; 93 [folio 7]. This is the smallest containing but 4 leaves.

- At St. Catherine's Monastery in the Sinai (quires 3-29; 95).

Sinaiticus can now be viewed as one manuscript. The British Library has produced a printed volume and a free online copy at http://www.codexsinaiticus.org/en/

The main advantage of the printed copy (the Hendrickson Publishers facsimile) "is its pin-sharp clarity of detail, a clarity which the online version just cannot give...... [and gives a] replication of the original in all its different colours, shades and hues." (Cooper, p. 68).

Simonides and Kallinikos had a great deal to say about the changes that befell the manuscript at Sinai.

Simonides Letter TWO: In 1844 I was again at Constantinople, and went to the island of Antigonus to see the Patriarch Constantius, and give him an important packet of MSS. I was received with his usual courtesy, and in the course of conversation I asked about my transcript of the Scriptures. He replied, «**Long ago, my son, I sent thy valuable work to Sinai**». **And twice have I seen it myself in the Library of Sinai, first in 1844 and then in 1852.** 1 asked the librarians how and whence the Library had obtained it. They having nothing to say (neither the first nor the second knowing anything about it), were silent, and I said nothing to them about the transcription; but **taking it in my hands found it somewhat altered in form, both externally and internally, for it had an older appearance than it ought to have had, and the MS. was defective in part. As I remembered the dedication to the Emperor Nicholas (which I had prefixed to the book in golden characters), and found that it had been taken out**.

Simonides Letter THREE: **In 1852** I saw it there **myself, and begged the librarian to inform me how the monastery had acquired it** but he did not appear to know anything of the matter, and I, for my part, said nothing. However, **I examined the MS. and found it much altered, having an older appearance that it ought to have. The dedication to the Emperor Nicholas, placed at the beginning of the book, had been removed.**

CHAPTER 6: FURTHER QUESTIONS

Simonides Letter TEN: Mr. Bradshaw's very proper and natural query - «How is it possible that a **MS. written beautifully, and with no intention to deceive, in 1840, should in 1862 present so ancient an appearance?**» -1 answer simply thus: -The MS. had **been systematically tampered with, in order to give it an ancient appearance, as early as 1852**, when, as I have already stated, it had an older appearance than it ought to have had; and from what I then was, I am not surprised that Mr. Bradshaw should have been deceived in his estimate of its age.

Kallinikos Letter ONE: I certified them that this MS. of the Scriptures is still preserved in Sinai (as thou also knowest), because **I saw it there with my own eyes when I was in the Monastery of St. Catherine in 1845 in the month of July**, and handled it with my own hands, and **found it very defective, and somewhat changed** and when I asked the reason, I understood from **Gabriel**, the keeper of the treasures, that **his predecessor had given the manuscript to a German, who visited the monastery in 1844 in the month of May**, and who having had the MS. in his hands several days, **secretly removed a part of it**, and went away during the time that the librarian lay ill, afflicted with a typhoid fever.

Kallinikos Letter FIVE: Evidently he knew not the abstraction of his work from the monastery in Mount Sinai. I read also at first this acrostic in it, «Simonides'entire work»: but, after two days, **the leaf containing this formal acrostic had been removed** - it being unknown, as yet, by whom this was done. I know too, still further, that **the same Codex was cleaned, with a solution of herbs, on the theory that the skins might**

be cleaned, but, in fact, that the writing might be changed, as it was, to a sort of yellow colour.

Kallinikos Letter SIX: And further, **I repeat, that the MS. in dispute is the work of the unwearied Simonides, and of no other person. A portion of this was secretly removed from Mt. Sinai, by Professor Tischendorf, in 1844. The rest, with inconceivable recklessness, he mutilated and tampered with, according to his liking, in the year 1859. Some leaves he destroyed, especially such as contained the Acrostics of Simonides; but four of them escaped him, viz., one in the Old Testament, and three in Hermas,** as I long since informed Simonides: many palaeographical symbols also escaped his notice, but I do not know whether these were eventually overlooked.

Kallinikos Letter SEVEN: And as regards the letters, I wrote them all. But Simonides wrote the Codex that was taken by Tischendorf from Mount Sinai, and which was corrupted by Tischendorf himself. Let therefore those give over that distort truth for the sake of worldly interest.

Hodgkin Letter SIX: ....It is somewhat remarkable that when inquiries were made in February, 1861, at Mount Sinai, by the Rev. W. W. Woollcomb, of Salford, about the Biblical MS. sent thence by Tischendorf to the Emperor, **the reply of the librarian was «that he knew nothing about the matter, that he never heard of any MS. being sent to the Emperor, or brought away by Tischendorf»**.

CHAPTER 6: FURTHER QUESTIONS

(5) THE *LATE* EPISTLE OF BARNABAS AND *LATE* SHEPHERD OF HERMAS AT THE END OF SINAITICUS

In the Introduction we saw that in **1855** Simonides presented a Greek copy of the apocryphal *Shepherd of Hermas* to Leipzig University. Shortly thereafter Tischendorf exposed it as merely a Greek translation of a late Latin copy. This was before Simonides and Tischendorf had gotten to know each other, and before the Sinaiticus broke.

In **1859** Tischendorf returned to Sinai to retrieve further portions of Sinaiticus. On its closing pages he found a nearly identical copy of the *Shepherd* that Simonides had presented at Leipzig – also a Greek translation of a late Latin copy. Seeing that it was in the *same* hand writing, with the *same* ink, and on the *same* vellum as in the preceding leaves he immediately understood the implications this had for the entire manuscript and went about to reverse his "views" on the *Shepherd* shown at Leipzig – It was old after all!

While we do not have the "drama" regarding the apocryphal *Epistle of Barnabas*, the situation is exactly the same. It is written between Revelation and *Hermas*. It is a Greek translation of a *LATE* Latin copy, and written with the *same* hand, *same* ink same and on the *same* vellum as the pages before (i.e. *Barnabas* like *Hermas* was an integral part of the codex).

Did I say there was no "drama"? In fact there was quite a lot. For example, once again Simonides "burst on the scene" with his extraordinary abilities (long before the controversy broke and while much of the above was going on!) by publishing in **1843** The Epistle of Barnabas in **eight versions**. A review of his book was published in *The Star of the East*, a newspaper of Smyrna, Turkey (1 August 1843). And, there is much more about *Barnabas*; see especially Daniels (pp. 316-326).

(6) THE ACROSTICS AND OTHER IDENTIFYING MARKS SIMONIDES PLACED IN SINAITICUS

Simonides Letter THREE: The corrections in the handwriting of my uncle I can, of course, point out as also those of Dionysius the calligraphist. In various places I marked in the margin the initials of the different MSS. from which I had taken certain passages and readings. These initials appear to have greatly bewildered Professor Tischendorf, who has invented several highly ingenious methods of accounting for them. **Lastly, I declare my ability to point to two distinct pages in the MS., though I have not seen it for years, in which is contained the most unquestionable proof of its being my writing.**

Simonides Letter SEVEN: If you understand the twofold significance of the note which exists at the end of the fourth column of the eighth page of the pseudo - Friderico - Augustine Codex [earlier name given to Sinaiticus at Sinai], you would repent of what both you and your patrons have stirred up against me inconsiderately.

Kallinikos Letter TWO: This Codex, my son, I saw several times, and particularly three of **the Acrostics which thou showedst to me at Athos** when I overlooked thee in that pleasant writing -room of thine.

CHAPTER 6: FURTHER QUESTIONS

The first reads thus - Κ.ʹιμωνιδου χειρ ιπιραιωσε με

The second - Κ. Λ. Φ.ʹιμωνδδου Μακεδονὸ εργον διαριστον ειμι

The third - ʹιμωνιδου το ολον εργον

I also saw the fourth and fifth, but do not remember them now; and also calligraphic symbols, and especially the numerous corrections, and corrections again of these, and annotations both of thyself and of thy uncle, by which I recognised thy work....

Kallinikos Letter SIX: And further, I repeat, that the MS. in dispute is the work of the unwearied Simonides, and of no other person. A portion of this was secretly removed from Mt. Sinai, by Professor Tischendorf, in 1844. The rest, with inconceivable recklessness, he mutilated and tampered with, according to his liking, in the year 1859. **Some leaves he destroyed, especially such as contained the Acrostics of Simonides; but four of them escaped him, viz., one in the Old Testament, and three in Hermas, as I long since informed Simonides: many palaeographical symbols also escaped his notice, but I do not know whether these were eventually overlooked.**

The opponents of Simonides were determined to find and remove these identification marks in the margins of his codex. For example see Daniels (pp.329-331).

CHAPTER 7
FROM WHAT DID SIMONIDES COPY?

With the exception of Vaticanus, Sinaiticus (frequently disagrees with Vaticanus) is like no other manuscript. It has no direct exemplars before or copies after. It has many readings that are totally unique to itself. To say that it is Alexandrian misses the point that its textual affinities are "all over the place". Its "stated purpose" was not that it be the basis for further translation but rather a "decorative" example of an early Biblical manuscript for the Tsar of Russia. And, Simonides believed this "stated purpose"! In fact, at Athos there was another factor at work. Note first what Simonides and Kalinikos said about the sources.

Simonides Letter TWO: And so **we straightway inspected the oldest MSS. preserved in Mount Athos** of the sacred writings referred to. I for my part carefully considered the questions connected with the best possible performance of the penmanship. And the learned **Benedict** taking in his hands a copy of the **Moscow edition** of the Old and New Testament (published at the expense of the illustrious **brothers Zosimas**, and by them presented to the Greeks), **collated it, with my assistance, with three only of the ancient copies, which he had long before annotated and corrected for another purpose and cleared their text by this collation from remarkable clerical errors, and again collated them with the edition of the Codex Alexandrinus, printed with uncial letters, and still further with another very old Syriac Codex; and gave me, in the first instance, Genesis to copy…..**

Simonides Letter THREE: I myself determined to begin the work, especially as my revered uncle seemed earnestly to wish it. Having then examined the principal copies of the Holy Scriptures preserved at Mount Athos, I began to practise the principles of calligraphy, and the learned Benedict taking a copy of the **Moscow edition** of both **Testaments** (published and presented to the Greeks by the **illustrious brothers Zosimas**), **collated it with the ancient ones**, and by this means **cleared it of many errors**, after which he gave it into my hands to transcribe. Having then received both the Testaments, freed from errors (the old spelling, however, remaining unaltered),

Kallinikos Letter TWO: That master and pupil of all guile, and all wickedness, the German **Tischendorf**, has unexpectedly rushed into thy net: for having inspected in **the common library** (where it was found a short time ago, and where it was placed by thy spiritual father **Callistratus** when he went to Alexandria) the Codex which thou wrotest at Athos, **some twenty-two years ago**, as a present to the deceased Emperor of Russia, Nicholas I, at the request of thy wise and distinguished uncle **Benedict,** and subsequently going to Constantinople after his death **gavest unfinished to the blessed Patriarch Constantius, who sent it to Mount Sinai by the Monk Germanus** of Sinai, whom thou knowest, and which was afterwards given to the **Hieromonachus Callistratus to be compared with the three old Codices of the Sacred Scriptures** (which thou knowest, and which are kept in the treasury), and was then disregarded because **thou didst not make thy appearance at the proper time** in Mount Sinai to transcribe it according to the earnest wish of the

CHAPTER 7: FROM WHAT DID SIMONIDES COPY?

Patriarch, **he has proclaimed it as genuine, and as the oldest of all the known Codices in Europe** of the Old and New Testaments.

Kallinikos Letter FIVE: For **I myself saw him with my own eyes, in February, 1840, writing it in Athos**; and, owing to the death of the head of the monastery, he left the work unfinished, and went to **Constantinople**, taking the Codex with him, which also he delivered to the illustrious patriarch **Constantius**, and he sent it to the monastery in **Sinai** by a monk of that house, named **Germanus**, whose subordinate still lives in **Athos** to attest the writer. **And the partiarch sent the Codex there, in order that the transcript might be compared with other copies of the Old and New Testament, and then be transcribed by the same Simonides, and sacredly presented to the Emperor of Russia**, on the part, not of the monastery of St. Pantaleemon, according to the original intention of Benedict, but on the part of the patriarch Constantius. On this account, the hieromonk **Callistratus**, a wise man, and companion of the same house, undertook the comparison of it, and **did compare it with other codices** of the same house, by command of Constantius, the patriarch. And he, **having partly corrected it, left it in the library awaiting the return of Simonides, the first calligrapher in Greece**. He not coming in good time, the work was altogether neglected, and remained in the common library of the monastery for some time: until Dr. Tischendorf (coming to the monastery in Sinai, in **May, 1844**, and spending some days there, and having examined the MS. carefully and suspecting it to be ancient), tore off a small part of it privately, and went his way...

In my book *Early Manuscripts, Church Fathers and the Authorized Version,* 356 doctrinal passages that are in the KJV, but either missing or questioned in the Modern Versions are tested against a wide range of manuscript evidence. The following results were found for these 356 passages in Sinaiticus and Vaticanus, and also for the corrections found in the margins of Sinaiticus:

- Sinaiticus is **against** the KJV Doctrinal Text: 290 to 58
- Vaticanus is **against** the KJV Doctrinal Text: 294 to 21
- Sinaiticus corrections **agree with** the KJV Doctrinal Text: 70-19

With one exception, no other Greek manuscript on my list goes against the KJV Doctrinal Text to such a catastrophic extent as Vaticanus (93% to 7%). For the rest of the so-called "Five Old Uncials" – A (Alexandrinus), C, D-05 and D-06; it is about 50/50 for and against the KJV Doctrinal Text. With the Latin Vulgate it is also 50/50 and may have influenced the corruption in the previous four manuscripts. Regarding the other 42 older manuscripts on the list (07 to 045), it is four to one in favour of the KJV Doctrinal Text.

The thousands of manuscripts kept in Greek Orthodox monasteries overwhelmingly support the KJV Text. Historically they have been the *keepers* of this Text. It would have been totally out of character for an Orthodox monastery to use anything for translation that would result in the huge changes found in Sinaiticus. Therefore we would not think that the Russian Orthodox *Moscow Edition* (published by Zosimas brothers in 1821) would be any different. Material on the *Zosimas Edition* that I have seen from Steven Avery confirms this (at least in the New Testament).

CHAPTER 7: FROM WHAT DID SIMONIDES COPY?

There is in fact another manuscript (of large enough size) that moves strongly against the KJV Doctrinal Text (5 to 1). It is in a different category of manuscripts known as the *papyri fragments*. *Papryi*[75] is said to be very old (early 3rd century), and because of its size and consistent support for Vaticanus is the most noteworthy among the papyri. Most accept these "facts" as merely part of the early history of the New Testament Text. Yet few realize that *Papryi*[75] has something else in common with Vaticanus. It has for some time been a favourite of the Vatican. Again, see Bill Cooper for a full expose' of the Vatican's involvement with this manuscript (pp. 95-103). Also, V (3) above.

CHAPTER 8
THE COLLAPSE OF THE MODERN VERSION TEXT:
NO COHESION, NO PROVENANCE, NO PROLIFERATION,
NO SINAITICUS AND PROBABLY NO VATICANUS

(1) AN ADMISSION

This heading to our final section states the matter perfectly! Even if the two "pillars" of the Modern Version Text were ancient manuscripts (they are not!), they and the forty or so manuscripts that are claimed as support results in only a *HOUSE OF CARDS*. The reason being - they give only partial support to Vaticanus and Sinaiticus, which in turn frequently disagree between themselves. This total lack of cohesion is in stark contrast to the manuscripts that support the KJV Text (at least 95% of the 5560 Greek manuscripts). Here there is only slight difference - just enough to let you know that they are independent witnesses to long lines of transmission that go deep into the past. That is, they are not merely direct copies of each other.

This hugely disproportionate amount of the variation among the few manuscripts supporting the Modern Version text is admitted by the editors of that text (the Nestle Aland Text). Barbara Aland and Klaus Wachtel write:

The papyri and majuscules are for the most part individual witnesses: despite sharing general tendencies on the forms of their texts, **they differ so widely from one another** that it is impossible to establish any direct genealogical ties among them. ("The Greek Minuscule Manuscripts of the N.T.", *The Text of the N.T. in Contemporary Research*, p.46. Emphasis mine).

(2) THE SINAITICUS PARCHMENT IS TOO SUPPLE

A basic point to keep in mind and despite Simonides' complaint of Sinaiticus being given "the appearance of age" (Simonides Letters TWO, THREE). Sinaiticus (and Vaticanus) appears to be quite an *"exceptional"* example of a manuscript retaining its *youthfulness* after the supposed 1650 years (a fact tacitly acknowledged since its acquisition by the British Library). Most manuscripts by this time would be stiff and brittle, as is the case with the 5th century Codex Alexandrinus (See Sorenson pp. 104,105). It is further noted that a parchment page ages from the edge and then inward resulting in uneven coloration. This is not seen on the pages of Sinaiticus (Cooper pp. 87-89).

CONCLUSION

FACT ONE: A young Simonides wrote Sinaiticus in good faith for the Tsar.

FACT TWO: The Vatican was the source of the corruption in Sinaiticus. By corruptions we do not mean the 50/50 doctrinal corruptions found in the Latin Vulgate or Codex Alexandrinus, but the sweeping (9 to 1 and 5 to 1) doctrinal corruptions found in Vaticanus and *Papryi*[75] - the attack weapon against the *Paper Popes of the Protestants*.

FACT THREE: Despite a rush to finish the project after Benedict's death; when the manuscript left Athos in 1840/41 it was **a *gift fit for a king***. This means that the numerous marginal corrections were not then in the codex. This means that the corruption of the text itself occurred while Simonides was penning the manuscript. This means that someone slipped the young Simonides a rogue manuscript that would bring it into line with Vaticanus. See for example Daniels' suspicions (p. 328). Note also that *Benedict* is not a Greek name but Latin. Questions were raised as to Benedict's identity and the different dates given for his death. Was there anything untoward in this? ***We do not know*** the identity of the Vatican "plant" or who was on the Vatican's payroll. But, with the basic facts before us, such a one had access to Athos. The fullest account we have leading up to the penning of the manuscript is the following that we have seen before:

> And the learned Benedict taking in his hands a copy of the Moscow edition of the Old and New Testament (published at the expense of the illustrious brothers Zosimas, and by them presented to the Greeks), collated it, with my assistance, with three only of the ancient copies, which he had long before annotated and corrected

for another purpose and cleared their text by this collation from remarkable clerical errors, and again collated them with the edition of the Codex Alexandrinus, printed with uncial letters, and still further with another very old Syriac Codex; and gave me, in the first instance, Genesis to copy. (Simonides Letter (Elliott pp. 55,56)

FACT FOUR: *Nothing* in Simonides' letters gives any hint of a plot. It was always to be a gift to the Tsar of Russia. He was simply the young penman and for a short time the courier. In **1840,41** he took it to Constantinople, ostensibly to carry it on to the Tsar. Constantius, however, after an examination urged it be sent to the library at Sinai. Surely this Greek Orthodox archbishop would have been alarmed at the strange readings in the New Testament. Either at Antigonus where Simonides next took and left the codex or at Sinai (more likely), the many corrections were placed in the margin of the manuscript. These overwhelmingly were in support of the Received Text. These *positive changes* were ignored and did not result in the already corrupted text being changed.

FACT FIVE: Tischendorf, funded by a Catholic king and subtlety "steered" by Rome arrives at the Sinai monastery in **May 1844** and finds an "ancient" manuscript. He removes 43 leaves out of the Old Testament and presents them to Kind Frederick. Tischendorf promotes the importance of his discovery. Shortly thereafter one Porphry Upensky of Russia published *The First Trip to the Sinai Monastery in 1845*. The manuscript is described as being *white* and *still white* in a further book in **1850** (Daniels p. 93). Its further *negative changes,* darkening ("aging") and perhaps the removal of the end of Mark took place before Simonides visit to Sinai two years later in **1852**.

FACT SIX: Simonides continues his trade and travels as a seller of "ancient" manuscripts. On a trip to Sinai in **1852**

CONCLUSION

he sees his manuscript *much altered with the appearance of age*. In **May 1859** he raises the question as to whether the manuscript Tischendorf discovered was in fact his own, At Liverpool in **1860** he is shown Tischendorf's facsimile and *immediately recognizes it as his own*. **Between 3 September 1862 and 26 Aug 1863** he entered into intensive correspondence with the British press (often *The Guardian*). Though attacked and derided on a wide front, his story did not change. At one point he challenged Tischendorf to meet him in a public forum. The meeting did not take place.

FACT SEVEN: By the end of 1863 interest in the story waned. Tischendorf and the revisers moved forward. Codex Sinaiticus received wide acceptance as an ancient manuscript. The Westcott and Hort Text based primarily on Sinaiticus and Vaticanus was published in 1881 and became the basis for nearly all translation thereafter.

After his last letters very little was heard of Constantine Simonides. It is said that he died in Egypt of leprosy. The date and the place are not known. There is little doubt that he did write Sinaiticus. There is little doubt that the Vatican corrupted it.

FACT EIGHT: With the huge effort and vast sums spent promoting the Modern Version Text; few from that side will rush to acknowledge the fall of Codex Sinaiticus. The vested interest in keeping it afloat is too great. Note one apparent example:

In **1844** Tischendorf took 43 leaves of Sinaiticus to Leipzig. These leaves were and are known to be *white* (Tischendorf said he saw "346 fine and fair leaves", Elliott p.10). In **2009** the British Library produced an online copy of Sinaiticus; in which the Leipzig leaves were *white*. In **2011** the British Library in association with Hendrickson Publishers published a facsimile; in this the Leipzig leaves were *no longer white*. We can only wonder whether a similar "adjustment" will be made to the online copy! (Thanks to Steven Avery for this alert).

Tischendorf "won the argument" and that with many honours bestowed and accolades at his funeral in **1875**. Simonides died of leprosy; we do not know when but somewhere in Egypt. He died totally discredited. His story "died" with him. *We do not think so*!

For nothing is secret, that shall not be made manifest;

neither any thing hid, that shall not be known and come abroad. Luke 8:17

PLEASE NOTE AGAIN: The sudden appearance and utter divergence of Codex Sinaiticus, Codex Vaticanus and Papyri 75 from the vast body of manuscript evidence, coupled with their *essential* agreement among themselves, demonstrates that they were not the product of accident or carelessness. This was a deliberate work!

J.A. Moorman, London, May 2018

INDEX OF WORDS AND PHRASES

1844 6, 11, 19, 20, 25, 31, 50, 64, 67, 70, 72, 93, 95, 110-112, 115, 119, 126, 127
1855... 11, 12, 24, 27, 28, 54, 113
1862 and 1863 6
350 AD 11
3500 people 5
356 doctrinal passages 120
80 per cent 5
A Biographical Memoir of Constantine Simonide 30
academic 13, 59
acrostichs 50
Aegina 46
Alexandria 11, 32, 37, 40, 54, 58, 61, 64, 67-69, 72, 73, 77, 78, 83, 105, 106, 118
Alexandrine Philological Catalogue 45
Alexandrinus .. 22, 33, 117, 120, 124-126
amusing 56, 78
ancient .11, 13, 16, 19, 21, 24-26, 28, 29, 33, 34, 43-46, 49, 51, 55, 66, 70, 101, 107, 111, 117-119, 123, 125-127
ancient manuscript 11, 16, 19, 25, 123, 127
antagonists 40, 79, 84, 89
Anthenaeum 29
Anthimus and Constantius .. 35, 103
anti-German attitude 14
Antigonus ... 31, 36-38, 103, 104, 110, 126
antiquarian 65
antiquity 11, 12, 15, 16, 22, 28, 39, 40, 57, 61, 66, 90, 99, 107
anti-Romanism 91

Apocalypse 22
apocryphal 12, 113
Apostles 96
apostolic fathers 23, 34, 101
appearance 32, 37, 41, 51, 65, 76, 106, 108, 110, 111, 118, 124, 127, 128
Archbishop ... 32, 54, 55, 94, 104, 107, 109
Archbishop of Libya 32
Aristeas to Philocrates 32
Athens 43, 46
Athos .. 24, 27, 33, 34, 36, 40, 43, 46, 49, 53-55, 57-59, 61-64, 66, 70, 87, 88, 91, 99, 101, 104, 105, 108, 114, 117-119, 125
audacious acts 13
Augustanus 19, 22, 25, 51, 77, 82, 85, 93, 99, 106
back-pedalling 13
Barbara Aland 123
bargain 5, 6
Barnabas 20, 23, 24, 34, 36, 101, 103, 113, 114
basket of papers 19, 25, 26
basketloads 19, 25
Bell 5
Benedict ... 33-35, 38, 43, 49, 61, 62, 64, 70, 86-89, 101, 103, 105, 108, 117-119, 125
benefactor 93
Berlin 28
Beyrout 72
Biblical manuscripts 27
Biblio.com 15
Bill Cooper 12, 17, 92, 121
Bodleian 28
Bradshaw 28, 51, 60, 61, 111

129

bribed 73
British Museum....... 5, 15, 28, 29, 52, 136
British press 6, 29-31, 58, 127
Brompton 81, 82
brother 36, 103
Cairo 20, 54, 65, 73, 98
calligrapher .32, 34, 70, 90, 102, 119
calligraphist ...12, 38, 39, 46, 114
Callinicus.............................. 52
Callinikos.............................. 50
Cambridge. 50, 51, 59, 60-62, 82
catastrophic......................... 120
Catholic 26, 92, 93, 126
Catlistratus........................... 32
Charilaos 46
Cheltenham.......................... 28
chief architect....................... 11
Chris Pinto..................... 17, 92
Chrysographer...................... 47
clean 35, 102, 108
Clement 23, 34, 101
Codex Frederico - Augustanus 19
Codex Sinaiticus.... 1, 2, 5-7, 11-16, 19, 26, 28-30, 34, 38, 40, 55, 60, 61, 76-80, 84, 85, 95, 106, 107, 127, 128
Coenobiac 88
cohesion.............................. 123
compilation 15, 62
Constantine Tischendorf.. 11, 12, 15, 25
Constantinople......29, 31, 35-38, 49, 55, 64, 65, 70, 89, 103, 104, 106, 107, 109, 110, 118, 119, 126
Consul..................... 65, 71, 106
controversy 11, 76, 79-81, 85, 88, 113
Cooper.13, 60-62, 92, 94, 95, 97, 98, 108, 109, 124

correspondence..... 15, 40, 54, 59, 80, 127
Countess Etleng............ 36, 103
Damascus............ 54, 67, 69, 91
Daniel Wallace...................... 17
Daniels.....62, 114, 115, 125, 126
David Daniels........................ 17
David H. Sorenson 17
Davies...................... 53-58, 106
Dean 62
diatribe................................. 87
Die Sinaibibel 19
Dindorf................................. 46
Dionysius .32, 34, 38, 39, 46, 47, 71, 86-88, 90, 101, 114
Dionysius the Areopagite 34, 101
discoverer 39, 57
discoveries........................... 85
dishonesty 13
Doutreleau 98
Dr. Tregelles .. 33, 34, 38, 40, 44
Drakakes............................... 50
eagerness of the friends of the Codex Sinaiticus................ 80
Early Manuscripts, Church Fathers and the Authorized Version 120
ecclesiastical ... 16, 47, 53, 56, 58
ecclesiastics.......................... 56
Egyptian hieroglyphics...........28
Egyptologists 28
eight versions..................... 113
Elliott. 14-20, 29-31, 33, 39, 40, 42-44, 46-53, 57-59, 62, 64, 67, 68, 72-74, 77-79, 81, 85, 86, 90, 92, 106, 126, 127
Emperor of the French............ 50
Epistle of Barnabas ..20, 23, 35, 102, 113
Esdras 50, 63, 105
evidence....17, 30, 38, 42, 44, 48, 49, 77, 79, 80, 86, 93, 107, 120, 128, 136

INDEX OF WORDS AND PHRASES

exemplars 117
expedition 19, 25
F.J.A. Hort 11, 13
facsimile 78, 95, 109, 127
facsimiles 38
faith of the public 80
fake 12
false 13, 14, 33, 61, 86
falsehoods 42, 45, 72
Farrer 62
faulty 24, 97
fifty pages 29, 62
forged voucher 78
forger 12, 29
Frederick Augustus II .. 26, 93, 94
Friderico ... 19, 22, 25, 48, 51, 77, 82, 85, 93, 99, 106, 114
Gabriel 64, 111
gazelle skin 21
Genesis 33, 43, 44, 117, 126
genuine 23, 29, 42, 55, 56, 65, 70, 76, 83, 106, 119
genuineness 52, 57, 72, 82
Germanus . 38, 64, 70, 106, 118, 119
gift 34, 43, 61, 99, 101, 109, 125, 126
Gordian knot 46
grammar 12, 97
Guardian ... 28, 31, 33, 39-43, 49, 50, 52, 53, 57-60, 67-69, 72, 73, 76-78, 80, 81, 85, 86, 88, 106, 127
hegoumenos 56
Heiligen Lande 19
Hendrickson Publishers 109, 127
herbs 71, 111
heretical 97
Hieromonachos 55, 61, 64, 67, 68, 69, 73, 79, 80
Hilarion 38, 63, 105
hoaxes 57
Hodgin 78, 79

Hodgkin ... 30, 59, 60, 63, 67, 74-78, 80-82, 85, 86, 90, 99, 112
holes 107, 108
Hort 13, 14, 60, 96, 98, 127
HOUSE OF CARDS 6, 123
Idiorhythmic 88
Ignatius 34, 101
illuminated 39
ink 12, 13, 22, 47, 49, 113
Irenaeus 28
Irons 81, 82
J.K. Elliott 11, 13-15, 75
James White 17, 92
Jehoiakim 18
Jesuit 92, 95, 98
Jesuit conspiracy 92
Journal of Sacred Literature .. 13, 20, 39, 50, 53
Kallinikos 16, 31, 40, 41, 52-55, 58-64, 67-69, 72, 73, 76-80, 82, 99, 104, 105, 110-112, 114, 115, 118, 119
Kallinkos 62, 74
Keeper of Manuscripts 5, 60
keeper of the treasures 64, 111
King Frederick Augustus of Saxony 19, 25
King James Bible 2, 6, 12, 135
Klaus Wachtel 123
Lampros 62
Lampros information 62
Latin ... 12, 23, 24, 61, 66, 98, 99, 113, 120, 125
Latin copy 12, 113
Latin Vulgate 98, 99, 120, 125
Latinisms 13
leaf 19, 21, 35, 71, 82, 83, 102, 108, 111
Leipsic text 24
Leipzig ... 12, 28, 62, 65, 73, 109, 113, 127
Leipzig University ... 12, 109, 113
Leipziger Zeitung 20, 95

131

leprosy......................27, 127, 128
Letter......91, 101, 105, 107, 108, 110-112, 114, 115, 117-119, 126
Lexicon....................................45
library........32, 35-37, 43, 49, 64, 69, 86, 97, 102, 103, 105, 106, 108, 118, 119, 126
Library 11, 28, 31, 60, 63, 74, 95, 98, 109, 110, 124, 127, 136
Literary Churchman ...40, 41, 49, 51, 53, 57-59, 68, 69, 72, 79, 81, 85, 86
living enigma 46
London........5, 22, 40, 51, 53, 57, 68, 74, 82, 89, 128, 135, 136
Luke 8:17........................128
Lutheran 93
Macedonia 53
Maggs......................................5
Manchester Guardian........13, 18
Mark 16:9-20.................95- 97
Mark Michie 17
Mathematics 46
Mayer Museum 30, 75
Mayer Papyri 80
Melchisedec 86-89
Minuscule 124
misspelling.............................97
Modern Version text.........6, 123
Mohammed..................69, 91
monastery......11, 19, 20, 25, 26, 32, 34, 35, 37, 38, 43, 44, 46, 50, 53-55, 59, 62, 64, 65, 67, 69, 71, 87-90, 92, 93, 101, 103, 104, 106, 108-111, 119, 120, 126
monks......26, 48, 54, 56, 73, 88, 92, 93
Moscow.........27, 33, 34, 54, 102, 117, 118, 120, 125
Moses Mount 21

Mount Sinai ... 19, 25, 31, 36, 37, 45, 52, 55, 57, 58, 63, 64, 67, 71, 73, 74, 85, 103, 105, 106, 107, 111, 112, 118
MS..21-25, 32-34, 37, 38, 43, 45, 50, 51, 57, 63, 69, 72, 73, 76, 78, 85, 92, 105, 110-112, 114, 115, 119
mutilated................72, 112, 115
Nestle Aland Text.................123
Newham.................................60
Nicander 63, 105
Nicholas ...32, 34, 37, 43, 50, 61, 63, 64, 101, 105, 110, 118
Nicholas I..................34, 61, 101
Niphon 63, 105
Notitia....................................19
Olynthiacs of Demosthenes......46
omission........................... 75, 97
one manuscript.....................109
opinions 50
opponents..52, 59, 82, 86, 87, 89, 115
Origen....................................23
Orthodox............91, 93, 120, 126
our mother 67, 91
palaeography.........22, 38, 66, 87
palimpsest.............................28
Panegyrics...............35, 102, 108
Panteleemon 34, 38, 101
Papal library............21, 25, 92
PAPER POPES 91
Papias 34, 101
Papryi[75]........................ 121, 125
papyri......... 45, 60, 98, 121, 124
Papyri 75 .... 98, 128
papyri fragments 98, 121
parchment 21, 22, 34, 35, 101, 103, 108, 124
partisan...............................77
Pastor of Hermas..................24
patriarch..... 36, 37, 70, 103, 104, 119

INDEX OF WORDS AND PHRASES

Patriarch Constantius..31, 38, 46, 64, 104, 106, 110, 118
Patrum Apostolicorum Opera. 13
Paul 23, 34, 101
peremptory 80
Phillips 28
photographs 108
Polycarp 34, 101
portions 11, 12, 19, 20, 22, 25, 28, 51, 59, 85, 113
preservation 5, 6, 50
Procopius 34, 101
Protestant 26, 93, 95, 99
Providence 16, 21
pseudo—monks 74
publish 31, 41, 63, 68, 69, 71, 99
pursue 15, 85
Queen Victoria 50
Reformation 91, 92
replacement 95
revised text 11, 99
Revised Version of 1881 ... 16, 60
Rhega 46
romantic story 15
Rossico 86, 88, 89, 90
Royal Society of Literature 80, 82
Russian 24, 34, 65, 71, 88, 93, 101, 104, 120
same scribe 95
Saxon Minister von Falkenstein 20
Saxony 26, 93, 94
scholars 12, 13, 27, 28, 58, 98, 99, 107
Scrivener 17
second pillar 11
Septuagint 19, 20, 25
Shephard of Hermes 12
Simonides 11-18, 24, 27-31, 33, 36, 38-42, 44, 48-55, 57-64, 67-69, 71-83, 85-91, 99,

101, 103-105, 107, 108, 110-115, 117-119, 124-128
Sinai 11, 12, 28, 31, 36, 38, 48, 52-54, 58, 59, 63-65, 69, 72, 91-93, 95, 99, 101, 103-107, 109, 110-115, 118, 119, 126
Soviet Government 5
St. Catherine 19, 20, 25, 63, 105, 109, 111
steer 93
Steven Avery 17, 120, 128
steward 20
Stewart 30, 31, 44, 46, 49, 78
story 11, 13, 14, 16, 18, 19, 26, 30, 33, 34, 61, 92, 127, 128
Stourtzas 36, 37, 103, 104
strange days 6
surreptitiously 56
Sydney Morning Herald 5
Symi 27
Syriac 33, 117, 126
tampered .. 51, 72, 111, 112, 115
tardiness 42
Tebizond 38
Telegraph of Bosphorus 88
tenuous 11
Text 6, 12, 13, 15, 17, 91, 92, 106, 120, 121, 123, 124, 126, 127, 135, 136
The Forging of Codex Sinaiticus 12, 17
third visit 20
thousands of manuscripts 120
thunderstruck 14
Tischendorfl 1-14, 16, 18- 20, 25, 26, 34, 38, 39, 42, 45, 48, 50, 51, 57-59, 61, 64-66, 69, 71-74, 77-79, 85, 92-96, 99, 105, 107, 112-115, 118, 119, 126-128
Traditional Text 17
transcription 32, 36, 103, 110

Tregelles...13, 14, 16, 34, 60, 61, 136
Trinity College........................ 59
truth 30, 38-40, 48, 52, 68, 71-74, 78, 84, 89, 90, 112
Tsar .. 91, 99, 101, 104, 105, 109, 117, 125, 126
two oldest New Testaments.... 11
typhoid fever....................64, 111
uncial...... 11, 33, 35, 60, 61, 102, 117, 126
University of Athens 62
Upensky.............................. 126
Uranius........................... 28, 45
Vatican 11, 21, 22, 24, 25, 92, 95-98, 121, 125, 127
Vaticanus 11, 15, 26, 90, 92, 93, 95-99, 117, 120, 121, 123-125, 127, 128
Vaux.. 60
vellum........ 12, 13, 19, 25, 26, 97, 107, 109, 113
verbatim................................ 98
waste basket........................... 11
West Derby...................... 78, 79
Westcott....................60, 98, 127
Westminster Dictionary of the Bible................................ 97
white..................... 109, 126, 127
Wilhelm Dindorf....................28
Woollcomb 85, 112
work of revision 11
worm 107, 108
Wright......41, 42, 50, 52, 59, 61, 63, 74, 77, 80-82, 84, 86, 87
write 35, 42, 44, 52-54, 56, 60, 67, 69, 70, 74, 82, 87, 91, 102, 108, 119, 123, 127
wrotest 64, 105, 118
yellow colour..................71, 112
Zosimas....33, 35, 102, 117, 118, 120, 125

ABOUT THE AUTHOR

Dr. J. A. Moorman and his wife, Dot.
2017

Jack A. Moorman studied for a while at the Indianapolis campus of Purdue University, attended briefly Indiana Bible College, and graduated from Tennessee Temple Bible School. He has been with Baptist International Missions Inc. (BIMI) since 1967 and has been involved in church planting, Bible Institute teaching and extensive distribution of Scriptures and gospel tracts in Johannesburg, South Africa from 1968 – 1988, and in England and London since 1988. He married his wife, Dot, on November 22 1963.

J.A. Moorman has written the following scholarly books defending the King James Bible and the Hebrew, Aramaic and Greek words that underlie it:

1. When the KJV Departs from the "Majority Text."
2. Early Manuscripts, Church Fathers, and the Authorized Version.
3. Forever Settled.
4. Missing in Modern Bibles—The Old Heresy Revived.

5. Samuel P. Tregelles—The Man Who Made the Critical Text Acceptable to Bible Believers.
6. 8,000 Differences Between the Textus Receptus and the Critical Text.
7. Bible Chronology: The Two Great Divides.
8. The Biblical and Observational Case for Geocentricity.
9. Revelation, God's Final Word.
10. Daniel, The Times of the Gentiles & of Jerusalem.
11. The Church; Beginning, Baptism, Body, and Bride.
12. Delivered From the Wrath to Come.

These well-documented works and are replete with evidence which he has gleaned from his own resources as well as references found in the British Museum, British Library and other libraries in South Africa and the United Kingdom.

He has been the pastor of Bethel Baptist Church in London, England since 1993. A great deal of his time, and on a nearly daily basis, is spent in distributing Gospel Literature on the crowded streets of London and beyond.